Success is a Given

READING THE SIGNS WHILE RE-INVENTING YOUR LIFE

Marlene Chism

ICARE Publishing

Springfield, MO

Success is a Given

ISBN: 978-0-9679411-5-8

Published by

ICARE Publishing
1223 W. Linwood
Springfield MO 65807
1.888.434.9085
www.ICAREPublishing.com

Cover and Typesetting by Susie Ward, The Admin Source

Re-invention requires the willingness to embrace change and the courage to leave the familiar comfort zone

This book is dedicated to all seekers who have the courage to re-invent.

"The first duty of love is to listen."
~Paul Tillich

Acknowledgments

The stories and examples in this book are real. The people you will read about come from all walks of life, from blue collar, to professional, to business owner to homemaker, however their names have been changed to respect their privacy.

I acknowledge with gratitude each person portrayed in this book whose struggles, challenges, failures and lessons are opportunities to learn more about life and to encourage others.

Thanks to my first book club, a group of women who encouraged me years ago to write a book. I'm grateful for the friendship of, Julie Reynolds, Paula Ringer, Michelle Kauffman, Sharon Huffman and Jacqueline Sanderson. Thank you for meeting with me each month, reading my writing and giving me feedback. You gave your time and knowledge without an expectation of getting a return. Thanks also to Deb Bostic and friends for being my second book group. This book is a result of the contribution you made to me out of the goodness of your hearts.

To my friends and family who love me for who I am instead of the roles I play, and who continue to encourage me through my many stages of re-invention.

I'm grateful for my husband who has witnessed my transformation from a factory girl to a professional speaker, to corporate trainer to author and business owner. No one realizes what "for better or worse" really means until you live with someone going through transformation and life invention.

I'm thankful for my team who make it possible for me to do what I love, thank you Betty, Tammie, Susie, and Caleb.

I acknowledge my clients who have used my products and services. Without you there is no business. Thank you for hiring me for speaking engagements, seeking my advice, buying my booklets, and inviting me back again and again. I'm honored to be of service to you.

Contents

"And the day came when the risk to remain tight in a bud was more painful than the risk it took to blossom."
~ Anais Nin

Introduction

"It is in your moments of decision
that your destiny is shaped."
Anthony Robbins

One day it hits you. Something needs to change. It might be your career, your marriage, your friendships or your identity. By your late thirties, it dawns on you that your life has already been invented. Some things are too late to change. You have made decisions about your education, your career, and your relationships and those choices led you to where you are today. Of course, you made these decisions when your main intent was to please your parents, make some quick money and satisfy your hormones. If you knew then what you know now, your choices would be different.

The restlessness you feel is a sign you are ready to enter the stage called "re-invention." Dissatisfaction is often a sign that change is needed. In fact, all your emotions are signs you can use to guide you to the next phase.

An interesting way to measure your growth is to look at what you are complaining about right now, whether that is your job, your spouse, or your current responsibilities, and remind yourself how happy you were at first to do the very thing you are currently complaining about.

Pay attention to your emotions and you will see the signs have been there all along, and include the full spectrum, from depression, anger, boredom, confusion, fear, apprehension, hope, excitement and joy. Examine any area of your life. The signals tell you where you are and what's going to happen.

For example, I remember how scared I was to leave my job of 21 years to re-invent my life as a speaker. I remember the apprehension of figuring out how to start a business and the hope of the possibilities in front of me. Then I remember how excited I was at first when someone called me for a free speech. I couldn't believe people actually wanted me to speak. I told all my friends. I practiced for hours and reworked the handouts time and time again. Looking back, I probably even bought a new outfit for the occasion.

Fast forward a few years. I had to turn down free speeches because I couldn't fit them in my schedule. Free speeches were no longer fun or challenging. I got bored with being just a speaker. I wanted to create products and build a business.

Most people sense some turbulence right before a major shift. You might feel crazy or off balance during this time of transition. Let me assure you, you're not alone. You are simply on the bridge between the last phase and the upcoming phase.

You might notice a pattern indicated by desire, excitement, fear, boredom, frustration, anger, and so on, back to desire. The common denominator is the emotional journey. The situation is only the vehicle for the lesson to be learned. Your emotions tell you the most about where you are in relationship to where you want to be.

Most of us are not very good at paying attention to our emotions, or we try to deny them or push past them

rather than seeing them for what they really are: a guidance system to tell you which direction you are headed
in any given set of circumstances.

The Emotional Scale

Visualize a vertical line. The top of the line represents all the good-feeling emotions such as joy, empowerment and love. The bottom of the line represents the
negative-feeling emotions such as grief, powerlessness,
and shame. Like swatches of paint in a paint store,
there are thousands of variations and degrees of any
one emotion which might range from stark white to the
blackest black.

Diagram of the Emotional Scale

Joy | Love| Empowerment
Enthusiasm | Happiness | Positive expectation
Hopefulness
Acceptance | Contentment
Boredom
Pessimism
Frustration | feeling overwhelmed
Anger
Hatred | Revenge
Insecurity | Unworthiness | Guilt
Grief | Powerlessness | Shame

Once you learn to identify where you are on the
emotional scale, you can use these signs to help you

on the journey of re-invention. In addition, your life becomes more interesting and you can stop judging yourself and start enjoying the success journey.

Over the years, I've interviewed and worked with all kinds of people: entrepreneurs, baby boomers going through a mid-life crisis, people who have been through some traumatic event and those who are simply dissatisfied with their current situation. All of these people have at least three things in common. First, they are in a life transition preparing to re-invent some area of their lives. Second, the emotional journey people take when in the midst of re-invention creates second–guessing, doubting and judging. Third, many people miss the other signs that would serve them in moving forward faster. These signs are life lessons.

You've heard the saying, "When the student is ready, the teacher appears." When life offers you a lesson, the purpose is to learn from the lesson so you don't have to repeat the lesson. Otherwise, you are also going to repeat the emotional journey that goes along with the life lesson.

During these transitions, it is easy to misinterpret the signs and retreat. You think because you feel scared that you must not be going in the right direction. The reality is that growth involves a measure of discomfort.

Or, you might believe that because your life is in chaos, your chances of success are over. On the contrary, your dissatisfaction or turbulent situation is a signal that you are getting ready for a significant shift. You simply have to be able to see the signs so you can adjust and avoid getting derailed by negativity.

That's why it is important not only to feel what you feel, but to look for the lessons as well as the signs of success, so that your decisions work to your highest good.

One compelling reason for writing this book is that very few people are willing to talk about what they really go through during times of change. Most people are afraid of being judged if they admit how scared they are, or if they talk too much about their desires, doubts and defeats. The purpose of this book is to let you know you are not alone. I have purposely shared parts of my emotional journey of re-invention in order to help you to identify some of the signs on your journey, while encouraging you to notice the signs along the way.

My hope is that you become more intuitive while reading your signs, and that you freely accept and own the success that has gotten you to this place. I hope you enjoy your emotional journey, and know that your success is not a matter of if or when, but it is a given.

CHAPTER ONE

The Search

"The journey of a thousand miles begins with one step."
Lao Tzu

The first sign that you are on the road to re-invention is that you start to search for something to make you feel happier. The search might be for a new job, a more exciting place to live or a better relationship. The search can be born of hope, or out of frustration because

> The purpose of life is a life of purpose."
>
> ~ Robert Byrne

you are stuck and wish for change. You have a good job, but you don't like it. Your boss is a jerk and your co-workers are incompetent. You have your health, but you don't appreciate it. You could go for a walk or do yoga, but you're not interested. You have a roof over your head, but it's not enough. You are no longer satisfied. You're stuck and can't see any solutions.

At other times, the search begins because your circumstances change: You lose a job or an important relationship. The kids are grown and you have an empty nest. You come face-to-face with old age or your own mortality. The problem is you can't define what it is that you want.

> Searching is a sign you are getting ready for another level of success.

One thing is for sure—what you have now isn't it. You're not sure if your boredom and lack of fulfillment stems from your relationships or your career, but for some reason, you are just generally unhappy. Your self-esteem plummets and you start to focus on your failures and disappointments. You compare yourself to everyone else and you always come up short. To compound the problem, you feel guilty because you know you have so much to be thankful for. You try to feel appreciation in the other areas of your life. Although you love your spouse and kids, you feel resentment.

You can't go to your friends for support because all you get is unwanted advice. If you hear another positive-thinking pep talk, you will literally gag.

Your escape is to daydream about the past, or create fantasies about the future. You keep looking for the fairy godmother to show up or the glass slipper to fit. In your quest for answers, you become confused and overwhelmed, so you begin the search. Is religion the answer? More education? You experiment with your religion or go to school and change your major at least three times, only to end up with a double major and then you realize it isn't enough. So you go back to get your masters degree, but feel inadequate because you don't have your PhD. You live in the "land of never enough" where peace eludes you and worry chases you. You meditate and journal, and as a last resort, you get counseling. You get married or get divorced. You move from the city to the country, and still you don't have the answer. You wind up at a book store with this book in hand, hoping to find some answers.

The good news is that searching is a sign that you are getting ready for another level of success. Then you go through a period of being stuck. I call this "the fence-straddlin' position." You don't like where you are, but you don't know what else is out there. Or if you do, you aren't motivated enough to change. The bad news

is, right before you get unstuck, you go through a turbulence that feels like your internal computer is being
rewired.

If you could just get a sign of what you are supposed to do, then you could make a decision and move
forward. You say a prayer and ask for guidance, hoping
for motivation.

What you may not realize is that the pain you are
experiencing is the sign you have been asking for. The
pain is the very motivation designed to move you forward. Whereas before, you were sort of stagnant and
on the fence regarding your decisions, this new "pain"
you are feeling will have to increase in magnitude so
you will be motivated enough to get unstuck.

Two Big Motivators

Only two things motivate anyone: pain and pleasure. We do things either to avoid pain or to gain pleasure. The only reason you are stuck on the fence with
your decision is because there's not enough pain to
move you off the fence and not enough pleasure to
keep you there. The interesting thing about pain and
pleasure is this: The thing that gives you pleasure today
may be the thing that gives you pain later on. Anyone
going through a divorce knows what I mean, and anyone wanting to change jobs also knows this truth.

When I was 18 years old, I got a job at a factory, and I was so excited. My factory job brought a "measure of pleasure" in that the job eliminated the pain of having no income. I was able to buy a house, support myself and meet my basic needs. But after a while, the same thing that gave me pleasure started to give me pain. Factory work is boring. You use your back more than your brain. There's not much room for creativity. You work by the same people every single day, doing the same repetitive motion work, day after day. You get two 15-minute breaks, and the best part of your day is when you look up at the clock and realize it's time to rotate!

I wanted something more, but I didn't know what it was. I didn't have enough pain to leave, but just enough to make me unhappy. I was in the fence-straddlin' position. I felt guilty for not being thankful for all my blessings. I had a roof over my head. I had a decent job, a 401K plan, and something to do everyday, yet I was growing increasingly dissatisfied. At the time, it didn't dawn on me that I should be thankful for this dissatisfaction. Now I refer to this painful process as "The Three Life Tragedies."

The Three Life Tragedies

The first tragedy is when you know you want something more, but you don't know what it is. Some people spend their entire lives in the first tragedy. You hate your current situation, but you don't have a clue what else would interest you, so you live life unhappy and confused. On the emotional scale, you register between pessimism and acceptance. Until there is hopefulness and a clear vision about what you want, nothing much happens.

The second tragedy is when you become doubtful. You finally know what it is that you want, but unfortunately, you don't believe it is possible. When you are in the second tragedy, you have a dream, but you don't believe in your own power to manifest the dream. People in the second tragedy believe in the lottery or the good fairy, or prince charming more than they believe in taking action.

> You can't dance when you're busy straddlin' the fence.

The third tragedy is when you know what you want, you believe it is possible, but you are afraid to do what is necessary. I was stuck for a long time in the first tragedy: knowing that there must be something more, but having no idea what it was.

It was my friend, Marsha, who helped me out of the first life tragedy and into the second one. One day after hearing me complain about being stuck with a factory job with no opportunities, Marsha asked me an important question, "What would you do if there were no limits?" After some hesitation I said, "I would be a dancer or a choreographer." She said, "That's not going to happen, you live in Springfield, Missouri, not New York, and you haven't had enough dance lessons. Besides that, you are in your mid-thirties...it just isn't going to happen. "Whew! I'm off the hook," I said sarcastically to Marsha, proving my point that there were no opportunities for me. "Not so fast," Marsha interrupted. "What is your second choice?"

"I would be a professional motivational speaker!" I replied. What is so interesting about these two answers is that I was not involved in any form of public speaking and I was not taking dance lessons, even though I said these were two things that I would do if there were no limits.

At least with these new insights, I now had some ideas of what I wanted. As Dr. Phil McGraw says, "You have to name it to claim it." The only problem is that in the second tragedy, you know what you want, but you just don't see how it is even remotely possible.

People are so incongruent. They talk about their dreams all day long, but then won't take one step toward fulfilling their dreams. Most people won't even go so far as to do what they love as a hobby because they think if they can't have it all, they won't have any of it.

Loving is a Sign

Pay attention to the emotions you experience when you love something. Loving something registers high on the emotional scale, right up there with happiness and enthusiasm, all the way to love and empowerment. If you love an activity, that is a sign that you should participate in that activity, even if you can only do it at the smallest level. That is also assuming what you enjoy doing doesn't infringe on anyone else's rights.

Doing what you love helps you to grow and discover other signs that will get you to your purpose and destination. At the least, new opportunities will open even if you only do what you love on the most basic level. Once the sign became clear to me, I joined Toastmasters, an international organization dedicated to the art of public speaking. People started saying, "You are so good. You could be a professional speaker." Slowly my doubts started to fade and the vision became more of a reality than a foggy dream.

Doing something I loved inspired me to make a decision. I would finish college and within two years, quit my factory job. However, as my quitting date drew near, suddenly my factory job didn't seem so bad. Doubts crept in. What if I was sorry that I quit? What if I couldn't figure out how to make a living? I was stuck right between the second and third life tragedy. I knew what I wanted and I believed it was possible, but moving into the unknown was scary.

The Transitional Tragedy

Between the second and third tragedy is a space where the pain that motivated you is the pain that will also keep you stuck. This is the "transitional tragedy" that I refer to as the fence-straddlin' position. You know you have the ability to move forward, but you also know that in doing so, you will have to give up lots of things, including the excuses you wore like an old pair of shoes. You register right at contentment and sometimes you slide down into boredom.

Fence straddlin' keeps you stuck in limbo. There isn't enough pain to make you want to leap, and there isn't enough pleasure to make you want to stay. Fence straddlin' keeps you busy with your drama and worry as you justify your position.

What is the sign of the transitional tragedy? "All talk and no action" indicates a person is in the transitional tragedy. There is lots of drama and dissatisfaction, but no real movement. How do I know? Firsthand experience. Right before I left my job of 21 years, here's how fence sitting manifested for me: I said to my friend, Sherry, "Well, I was going to quit at the end of the year, but there's no reason not to wait until the New Year." Then once the New Year arrived I said, "Well, I think I'll go ahead and try to get my four weeks' vacation in before quitting." Finally, Sherry was tired of the excuses and she said, "You are never going to leave. You will be here talking about leaving for the rest of your life." Sher-ry's statement made me realize that you can't dance when you're busy straddlin' the fence. If you straddle for too long, you spiral down into frustration and even feel guilty for not stepping up to the plate.

Pain Is a Motivator

Luckily, there was more pain around the corner that helped me make my decision. Without much choice, I was farmed out on Friday nights to do sanitation in-stead of production. Sanitation meant cleaning the equipment, and since it was a food plant, we scrubbed the equipment until it sparkled. My new sanitation job was on the third floor where the pasta was cooked. The temperature was over 100 degrees and it stunk. The workers always had red faces dripping with sweat. The heat, stench and team combined reminded me of those pictures of hell you saw in a comic book as a kid. Work-ing in the heat was terribly uncomfortable, yet I would say, "I can do anything for eight hours." Obviously I have a high pain tolerance!

The fear of moving forward was so tremendous, that even with the new opportunities in front of me, no amount of dissatisfaction with my current position was enough pain to make me want to move forward. Any time I considered quitting, new questions came to mind: How could I consider giving up a steady income and my 401K? What if quitting turned out to be the wrong decision? I continued to sit on the fence.

The Power of Vision

My vision of moving forward started to diminish. That is, until there was a retirement dinner to attend. Ordinarily, attending retirement dinners was quite pleasurable. We got an extra 15 minutes for break and the company catered in a big buffet. However, this day a new and painful vision emerged in my mind.

I saw myself at the age of 65 or 70 years old and a big retirement cake coming toward me in my mind's eye. I visualized myself sitting there in my uniform and hairnet as everyone said their good-byes and scurried back to the factory lines. I saw myself looking at my gold retirement watch, knowing I had given up the best years of my life because of my fears of moving forward. It was that pain that motivated me to give my notice and jump off the fence of indecision.

Pain is not always the enemy. Pain can motivate you to change your current situation and seek solutions. When you say a prayer for guidance to move you forward, pay attention to the discomfort of your current situation, because that is your prayer being answered. When you experience any type of pain, be it dissatisfaction with your current situation, boredom, or restlessness in your relationship, count that pain as a friend that will push you off of the fence of stagnation and open up new opportunities for you.

SIGNPOSTS ▶

1. What was once exciting is now ordinary.

2. You feel as though something is missing.

3. You long for something more meaningful.

4. You recall things you used to like to do.

5. You get stuck for a while until you notice the sign of pain.

6. It becomes easy to define what you don't want.

7. You go through the three life tragedies.

   a. You want something more but don't know what it is.

   b. You define what you want but don't believe it's possible.

   c. You know what you want and believe it is possible, but fear keeps you stuck.

8. You are willing to take action.

9. Pain becomes the friend that motivates you to change.

Searching is a time of exploration that can be exciting and scary at the same time. One thing is for certain, you will experience a fair amount of confusion, discomfort or emotional pain when you are searching. Consider this pain your "flu shot." Remember what your mother said to you as a child, "It will only hurt for a little while." Understand that sometimes a little pain is necessary for healthy growth. It's also helpful to remind yourself that with it comes to personal growth, comfort is not a requirement.

CHAPTER TWO

The Comfort Zone

"Life shrinks or expands in proportion to one's courage."

Anais Nin

Another sign of growth is the chaos and confusion you feel right before you make the decision to jump off the fence. I have interviewed hundreds of people who are on the success journey of growth, and they all agree that right before a big transition or growth spurt, there is a dark night of the soul, the winter before the spring, the turbulence I have already referred to.

This turbulence is part of the cycle. Once you know this, you don't succumb to deep, dark depression. You might feel some instability and withdraw for a time, but ultimately, you understand the cycles of growth. All of nature, including your life, is about growth and expansion; therefore, if you are not expanding, you are dying. When you resist the natural cycles of expansion, it's because you are afraid to expand your comfort zone. You don't want to experience the natural discomfort that growth requires of you.

> If you are always comfortable, you probably aren't growing. If you are always uncomfortable, it means you are either getting ready for a transition or you are growing too quickly.

Resistance is Fear

We resist expanding the comfort zone, either because we fear the risk, or because getting one thing often means giving up something else. If you have a job with full benefits and a retirement plan, you may have to give up some of your ideas about security if you want to become a business owner. If you are single and desiring marriage, you have to give up seeing other people, leaving your dirty laundry on the floor or other habits that do not take another person into consideration. If you need to do something bold, you have to give up your story about why you aren't good enough, why it will always be this way, or why you are too shy, not smart enough, came from the wrong side of the tracks or whatever else is keeping you comfortably stuck in your little safe box.

Most of us resist change and personal growth because, intuitively, we know growing is going to require a fair measure of discomfort. Let me be clear on this: If you are always comfortable, you aren't challenging yourself and you aren't really growing. On the other hand, if you're *always* uncomfortable, then it means you are growing too quickly or you are stagnant and afraid of the change. My friend Sonja calls it being "one step away from crazy" when you are growing too fast.

One Step Away From Crazy

In less than two years' time, Sonja got a divorce, moved, married a man from a foreign country, got pregnant, had a miscarriage, got pregnant again, had a baby and got a new job. She said when she was going through these changes, she felt like she was "one step away from crazy." Sonja said if the lines weren't painted on the street, she wouldn't even know where the boundaries were. I tell you this to reassure you that if you are growing too fast, you'll have a mini-breakdown and you'll feel crazy. Rest assured you are not alone. You just need to step back a little so you can expand your comfort zone, but not be so far away from it that you feel one step away from crazy.

When you are not growing fast enough and feel stuck, your emotions will reside on the opposite end of the spectrum. Instead of feeling anxious and crazy, you feel depressed and hopeless. You are most likely stuck in the first life tragedy: knowing you want something more, but you're not sure what it is.

Nonetheless, we are always striving to find relief from the discomfort of growth or the despair of stagnation. Any type of pain or discomfort is ultimately nothing more than your emotions guiding you to valuable information. It's up to you to interpret that information and make the appropriate choices.

It was a measure of pain that helped me to leave a job that had become unsatisfactory. Leaving also meant brand new versions of pain, like the discomfort that comes with any learning curve as you develop new skills. Entering the business world fresh from the factory floor, it didn't take long to learn that growth and change aren't always fun. At first it seemed that I was a pioneer in a foreign land, and I kept looking for signs to let me know if I was on the right track or not.

You Are a Pioneer

In a real sense, all of us are pioneers in our own lives. Another way of saying it is, "We are all dancers learning new steps." It took lots of practice before I learned some of the steps that would later come in handy in building a business. In the beginning, I felt like a blind man with a cane searching for the next curb. For example, the world of networking was foreign to me, and I missed so many opportunities because I simply didn't see them unless I "bumped into a curb." A few times I stumbled or even fell down. When you are learning something new, you will make plenty of mistakes.

Now I'm thankful for the mistakes because they make great stories in my speeches, and I have realized that when it comes to growth, comfort is not a requirement.

> Any type of pain or discomfort is ultimately nothing more than your emotions guiding you to valuable information.

Comfort is Not a Requirement

The first national conference I attended was for the Association for Women in Communications. I went to this conference on some good advice from friends who said, "If you want to make it as a national speaker, you need to network nationally." I was also told, "Position yourself," and "You may get business" and "You may find a mentor." So I went with the intention of positioning myself, finding business and perhaps getting a mentor. However, once I got to the conference, I realized that I didn't know how to do those things. It was quite miserable being amongst established professional women. Looking back, I see I had a lot of feelings of unworthiness and my emotional scale ranged from insecurity to frustration and pessimism. This was before I knew anything about the emotional scale, or how life offers the perfect signs and lessons when you are re-inventing.

Life offered me the opportunity to sit by the most accomplished people in the place. Instead of seeing it as a sign of better things to come, I wanted to leave. Instead, I created a mantra and repeated it to myself, "Comfort is not a requirement." I said this over and over again when I felt the urge to bolt. That mantra became my salvation as I suffered in silence.

On last evening of the Clarion Awards dinner, I happened to sit by two women. One was from Washington, D.C., and the other from Atlanta, Georgia. Of course, they were both Clarion winners, which made the situation all the more intimidating. My first urge was to excuse myself and go back to my hotel room, but instead I silently repeated my mantra, "Comfort is not a requirement." I reminded myself that no one else needed know that I was uncomfortable. I nervously made small talk trying to divert the attention back to them so that I wouldn't have to talk about myself. Then, out of the blue, the woman from Atlanta said, "You look beautiful tonight."

"Thank you," I said, offering her nowhere to go in the conversation.

Then the woman from D.C. said, "Are you having a good time?" To which I replied, "No, actually I am quite miserable, but fortunately for me, comfort is not a requirement."

You can imagine the looks on my dinner partners' faces. I was mortified, but the point is, you have to start somewhere, and I was doing the best I could at the time. Now this becomes a funny story at some of my talks. You have to expand your comfort zone if you want to advance. Now I love going to conferences and I enjoy meeting new people. I would have never known this joy if I would not have been willing to go through the challenges of re-inventing my life.

The Value of Relationships

There are many lessons on the journey of re-inventing your life, and one of those is the value of relationships. No matter what you want to do, your success is going to manifest partially because of other people. You can have the best product or service, but if people don't know about you, then you won't get sales. I call this "being good in a closet." You are good at what you do, but no one knows about you.

Many people want to transition into a different kind of business, but have no idea how to sell or how to build business relationships. Many entrepreneurs believe if they have a good idea, the money will follow. However, until you build a foundation of relationships to help you promote, refer and sell your products, you won't make it. The problem is often a lack of relationship skills.

Seeing Yourself Clearly

I've seen more talented people fail because they didn't perceive themselves the way others perceive them. They are good at what they do, they know what they want, and they even believe it's possible, but they still lack interpersonal skills to move the process forward. You see, getting what you want isn't always about belief, action or knowing what you want. Sometimes it's about uncovering skills that still need to be developed.

For example, those who think they are the best communicators are often the worst. Haven't you known someone who wouldn't let you get a word in edgewise? That person thinks he's a great communicator, but most people feel bored when they are in his presence. It's always the guy who talks non-stop about himself, telling jokes with a lampshade on his head that thinks he's the good networker. Or the guy with two left feet that thinks he's the "Lord of the Dance." Part of personal growth is looking in the mirror to see what others see. Another part is being willing to learn the necessary skills.

Let me parallel two concepts: There is a vast the difference between shaking your bootie to some music versus learning organized dance patterns, steps and rhythms of a choreographed dance. There is also a vast difference between strutting yourself in a drunken stupor at a social event versus building quality relationships at a business function. The point I'm making is that many of us can't see what is so obvious to others because we keep saying, "I'm already a good dancer," or, "I'm already a master networker." There's a difference between knowing and doing.

Years ago there was an episode on "Seinfeld" that is often referred to as "The Dance Episode." You might have a chance to see it if you ever watch reruns. The character Elaine dances at a party and she thinks she's good, but everyone else is appalled at the way she sticks her thumbs up in the air and the awkward way she uses her elbows to gyrate to the music. As a TV audience member, you laugh along with her friends who see Elaine differently than she does herself. For all of her efforts to be a good dancer, the joke is on her. This episode in particular is a good example of the truth that often we don't see ourselves like others see us.

> Learning a new skill is a lot like dancing. At first, you won't be the best. You will make mistakes. You will appear to be clumsy, but you get better with practice.

To be good at any skill, it takes rehearsal and discipline until you become competent. If you are re-inventing any part of your life, you must commit to develop the skills required to move you to the next level. Just like dancing, you must build upon the foundation. At first, you won't be the best. You will make mistakes, you will appear to be clumsy and you will get better with practice.

Practice Makes Perfect

Conferences are the "dance floor" of business meetings and serve as a great way to practice. A side benefit is that you may never again see the people you just practiced on. I got lots of practice my first few years because I attended as many conferences as possible. I knew I was getting better, so I was ready to use my new skills. What I didn't know is that no matter how good you are, you probably still have things to learn. That's why it's important to just keep practicing.

> Conferences are the "dance floor" of business meetings and serve as a great way to practice.

It was my first time to Norfolk, Virginia, and my first workshop with National Speakers Association. It is exciting to be among hundreds of speakers, some relatively unknown and others who are like celebrities, at least in the speaking industry. Because conventions can be intimidating, I made a commitment to always make the effort to be the first to speak and introduce myself. Part of my discipline was to seek out people who look a little lost, and I happened to spot such a gentleman after finishing my registration.

He was an attractive man of average build with a well-kept beard and conservative clothes. Honestly, he looked a bit like a computer nerd, or a college chess champion: the quiet, intelligent, shy type, very left-brained. I've always been impressed by those who seem to have the high IQ but no social skills, so I sat down and introduced myself.

"Hi, my name is Marlene Chism."

"Ric Edelman," he said as he extended his hand. We continued our small talk on the first level communication that tends to break the ice: looking for commonalities and talking about the weather.

"Is this your first convention?" I asked.

"Yes," he answered.

"Well, I'm kind of green and don't know the big dogs from the wannabes," I said, trying to be charming and witty.

"Well, by looking at the schedule, there isn't anyone here of any status. Either that, or I don't have a clue," he chuckled.

"Well, I guess you don't have a clue!" I responded, assured of my superior knowledge. Anyone in the speaking business who doesn't know Patricia Fripp or Nido Qubein is obviously from Mars. I could tell by the way he laughed sheepishly, he recognized that I'm not such a greenhorn after all.

Then we moved on to level two of conversation, fact disclosure. We started talking about our speaking topics. He speaks on financial planning and investing; my topic is communication and relationships. Just as I thought, he was my direct opposite. He was dressed in brown (boring) and I had on red (exciting). He seemed aloof and I'm high strung. I sympathized with him on how tough it is to make a dull subject interesting. After all, how exciting could financial planning and insurance be, especially when you compare it to my **fun motivational programs and networking seminars?**

I could tell just by looking at him he was a little, well, boring, or perhaps "dry" is a better word. I sensed that he thought I was a tad flighty, but I was certain he appreciated me taking him under my wing nonetheless. Then I moved into level three conversation, opinion giving.

I told him how to be more interesting as I amused him with stories of how I occasionally tap dance in motivational presentations. (Was he rolling his eyes when I said that, or was that just a speck in his eye?) He gave me his opinion about how I wasn't using QuickBooks efficiently. "Oh well, that's just him trying to show me how smart he is," I thought to myself. I told him about my audio tape that was almost finished and gave him guidance on how to use products as a way to leverage and negotiate.

Why were people staring at us? I wondered. Then out of the blue, one of the gawkers approached him, stuck out his hand and said, "Mr. Edelman, you are my hero," or something to that effect. I observed as they vehemently shook hands.

"I listen to your radio show every chance, and I watch you on TV when I know you're on, and hey, man, I loved your last book!" his worshiper continued.

What? Radio show, TV—book? Who is this guy?

When I got home I looked at Mr. Edelman's website. It was a top-of-the-line website with financial calculators, testimonials from those who had read his New York Times bestseller, and info about his upcoming radio and TV appearances. Apparently Ric Edelman is a financial guru in Virginia, and come to find out, he was soon to be on "Oprah" to share his wisdom. Boy, did I ever feel like Elaine on "Seinfeld"!

The story doesn't end there. I got a chance to reconnect with Ric Edelman a few months later. Our local newspaper was doing short informational spots on websites. *The Springfield News Leader* would interview a person and ask that person what was their favorite website. Along with the interview, they printed a picture of the website and a picture of the person whom they interviewed.

I was asked to be an interviewee. Being such a savvy networker, I didn't want to pass up an opportunity to redeem myself, so I said, "My favorite website is Ric Edelman's. It has financial calculators and great advice for anyone who wants to become a better money manager." I knew that would make me seem very smart to the readership. Then as a side note, I told the person interviewing me, "Ric is really sarcastic in his approach, but his tips are good."

> If I were learning to dance, I would say that I was definitely looking quite clumsy, but I was persistent in working to refine my steps.

Guess what was in the paper? Only the part about him being sarcastic! If I were learning to dance, I would say that I was definitely looking quite clumsy, but I was persistent in working to refine my steps. I decided to go ahead and clip the article and send a handwritten note to Ric, thinking that he might just get a laugh out of seeing his information in our local newspaper. I reasoned that he knows he is sarcastic. He's from the East Coast. I shouldn't have said something about him behind his back if it wasn't something I was willing to say in front of his face. About two weeks later, I got a nice handwritten note from Ric saying that his staff was laughing all the way down the hall. Then he wrote a little tongue-in-cheek message that read, "Sarcastic, me? Never."

Fast forward another year, and who do I see on "Oprah"? Ric Edelman, who successfully avoided a cat fight with two women arguing over whether it is a good investment to put a second mortgage on a house, or something to that effect. Once again, I attempted to connect with Ric by emailing him a short note about how well he handled the two women on the "Oprah" show. I asked him if he remembered me, to which he charmingly replied, "How could I forget someone as interesting as you?" (Or was that a hint of sarcasm?)

SIGNPOSTS ▶

1. New experiences become more important than the comfort zone.

2. To get something else, you are willing to give up certain things.

3. You become a pioneer in your own life.

4. It seems like you are taking dance lessons with two left feet.

5. People occasionally laugh at you.

6. Learning from your mistakes is the payoff for discomfort.

7. You start getting better with practice.

My beginning experiences have taught me many lessons. When meeting new people, listening is always better than talking. It's more beneficial to be impressed than to try to impress others. Assumptions are dangerous and can make you look foolish. When you speak with authority, first you should really know your audience. Don't say anything about anyone that you aren't willing to tell them to their face.

Finally, learning to build relationships is a lot like learning a new dance. At first you won't be the best. You will appear to be clumsy and you get better with practice. When you are willing to expand your comfort zone and do "your work," you start attracting all kinds of wonderful circumstances that you never even dreamed possible. Being in this flow is the result of right beliefs, right thinking and right action.

CHAPTER THREE

The Law of Attraction

"Success is getting what you want.
Happiness is wanting what you get."

Dale Carnegie

One of the most exciting signs you will see on your journey is the sign of the Law of Attraction: What you want also wants you. You must look for the evidence that this is true. When this becomes your belief, you'll stop straddling the fence and you'll take action much more quickly.

Before you understand how to read Law of Attraction signs, you will unconsciously fall for the belief that you have to figure it all out first before taking any action. This is because you haven't yet learned how to look for evidence that you can have what you want and it doesn't have to be difficult.

Instead, you are looking for evidence about what you still don't have and you are constructing reasons why you can't have what you want. These mind patterns keep you from taking inspired action. Another reason you fail to take action is that you are so worried about "doing it right" that you spend needless hours pouring over all the rules instead of trusting the process.

The fear of "doing it wrong" keeps most of us from really stepping out to claim what is ours. It's like being afraid to dance because you think everyone will make fun of you. Most of us would rather be right about our inability to get what we want than to risk looking stupid trying to get it. If I have said it once, I have said it a thousand times, the need to be "right" keeps you stuck.

> The need to be "right" keeps you stuck.

By striving for perfection instead of moving forward, you fool yourself into believing you are willing to do the work. Truth is, you are afraid of going for it and you

are scared to death of looking stupid. It's too hard to
believe that what you want also wants you. That is why
it is important to hold this thought in mind and then
look for the signs to prove it true.

The Story Keeps You Stuck

Once stuck, your own thoughts will reinforce your
beliefs that you don't deserve to get what you want and
you will come up with all kinds of reasons why life isn't
fair, or why you can't meet the love of your life, or why
you can't develop a successful career. This will become
the story you live your life by. You will come up with
sayings like, "There are only so many opportunities,"
or, "It's more difficult because I'm a woman," or, "If I
was of a different race then I'd have it made," or my
own personal mantra,
"I have to figure it out."
The need to figure it out
can make life so much
harder than it is if you
would just lighten up
and trust the process.

> Look for evidence that
> indicates a different
> truth: What you want
> in life also wants you.

Look for Evidence

Look for evidence that indicates a different truth:
What you want in life also wants you. You don't even
have to figure it out, you just need to claim it and then
do the next right thing. I learned this valuable lesson

when I was finishing a business trip in New York City and my friend Julie had joined me for a few days of fun in the Big Apple. The fun was intermittently interrupted by the frustration of learning to travel in a big city.

Growing up in the Midwest certainly hadn't taught me or Julie how to hail a cab in New York City. The embarrassment of having my incompetence on display seemed only to increase my aggravation as we waited on the corner of Fifth Avenue and 32nd Street watching a woman appear out of nowhere to slither into the cab that we had just hailed. "If I could just 'figure out the rules' of getting a cab in New York City, we'd be out of the rain and on the way to our hotel," I said to Julie.

It looked so easy watching everyone else, I remember rehearsing over in my mind the things I once heard about hailing a cab. "Does a bright light mean he is on duty or off duty? Does it mean he already has a passenger or is looking for a passenger?" I asked myself. Is there a best time of day to catch a cab, or a certain way to stand to get their attention?

I analyzed the situation, determined to figure it out as I continued to observe the savvy, cab-hailing people who live in New York seem to instantaneously manifest a cab just by thinking about it.

So far, I had learned of several things that didn't work: Standing timidly on the corner and waving like a 5-year-old who just saw Santa only got me a few friendly waves from cab drivers who already had passengers. Apparently, my politeness was neither noticed nor appreciated. "Waiting my turn" didn't seem to register with the street-savvy New Yorkers who don't believe in "first come, first served," but operate more on the basis of "every-man-for-himself" kind of philosophy. While I was trying to "figure it out" it happened again! A New Yorker slithered in front of me and took the cab that I thought I had hailed.

> Life isn't always fair: sometimes people steal your cab and laugh at you while they're doing it, but that shouldn't stop you from learning from them about how to get a cab.

"She stole our cab! How dare she jump in ahead of us! That's so rude! It's not fair!" I exclaimed to Julie.

"She's also laughing at us," Julie added in an almost melodic voice as we watched the cab speed away with nary a concern that we had waved it down first. This new "learning experience" didn't seem to affect Julie the way it did me, and that even aggravated me further. "That's interesting," Julie said as she watched three more cabs pass us by. Julie's "interest" in our current situation only seemed to fuel my fire. I felt the need to get agreement from Julie.

"I'm furious," I reiterated, trying to convince her of the severity of the situation as we stood in the pouring rain, luggage in tow, only to be passed by again and again.

"Don't be angry," Julie said. "Let's look this experience as a way to quit resisting 'what is' and a chance to watch other people so we can learn what to do."

"I don't want to learn, I just want a cab to pick us up and get us out of this nasty rain!" I shouted over the traffic noise. Eventually, I saw someone writing a check to pay for their cab ride, and that indicated to me that since people were actually getting out of the cab it might benefit the driver to get another passenger.

So without much hesitation I slid into the cab before the financial transaction was completed. However, even though I was successful in getting a cab, I knew that it was only luck that I had noticed the opportunity. I was determined to do it the "real way" by competing with other people on the street to see if I could get one first.

> Life always gives
> you opportunities.

Life Gives You New Opportunities

Life always gives you opportunities, and our next opportunity came the day we were heading back home. I had a sense of determination mixed with dread, and I expressed this to Julie. "Okay, here we go again. This time I'm going to really step out there even if I look stupid!" After a couple of attempts, we still had no luck.

"Should I walk back to the hotel to ask the concierge to help us? I can pay him $5 to get a cab," Julie said, almost cowering at my impatience. The thought of wasting $5 to do something as simple as hailing a cab was something I simply could not allow.

"Absolutely not!" I screamed. "Five dollars buys a large Strawberry with Chocolate Dip Dairy Queen Blizzard! I'm going to hail a cab if it's the last thing I ever do in New York City!"

In my fury, I boldly stepped off of the curb and stuck my hand out like I was hailing Hitler, and voila! A cab came almost immediately to pick us up. "Now that's more like it," I thought to myself as I gave a satisfied nod to Julie. It appeared that Julie was quite impressed with my new cab-hailing savvy.

"LaGuardia Airport," I said to the cab driver as I winked smugly at Julie. The cab driver's eyes were dead and his expression gave no indication of what he thought about taking us to the airport.

"Did I just ruin your day? I mean, when you go to the cab drivers' convention, do they tell jokes about someone from the Midwest hailing a cab, and then when you find out they are going to LaGuardia, does everyone moan and laugh at the punch line when you say you wish you had hung yourself instead?"

"No, I'm glad you are going to the airport...it's more money for me," he said without cracking a smile.

"Well, I couldn't tell by the tone of your voice," I said straining to see his expression.

"That's a good thing, to take someone to LaGuardia on a Sunday," he affirmed.

"Then you should smile, this is your lucky day," I continued.

It's hard to know why cab drivers don't want to chat. "You would think they would welcome a little human interaction," I thought to myself. It amazes me that you can sit in the same space with someone and only utter three phrases: "LaGuardia. That is $30.00, and thanks." Now my new goal was getting the cab driver to chat and to learn something at the same time.

I asked the cab driver a few questions: "So, what are the rules of hailing a cab? When your light is on, does that mean you are on duty, empty, full, or is that just for decoration? I keep trying to figure it out, but I still don't really understand. What are the rules for hailing a cab in New York City?"

Without taking a breath, or a moment to ponder, the cab driver said," You don't need to figure out anything. There are over 12,000 cabs in New York and we are all looking for you. Just raise your hand." Hmm. There are 12,000 cabs in New York that are looking for me. What I want also wants me! My scarcity-consciousness had me

> I made getting a cab much harder than it really is. How often do we do this same thing with big life goals?

believing that there weren't enough cabs to go around and only the savvy travelers were able to hail a cab. I made getting a cab much harder than it really is. How often do we do this same thing with big life goals?

SIGNPOSTS ▶

1. Analyzing and trying to figure it out is exhausting.

2. You learn what doesn't work.

3. You get angry when you see others getting what you want.

4. Anger motivates you to action.

5. It seems possible that what you want also wants you.

6. The seeds of trust start to take root.

7. Life lessons occur in almost every situation.

8. Action often leads to results.

Life isn't always fair, the way we judge fairness, or is it? Sometimes people steal your cab and laugh at you while they're doing it, but that shouldn't stop you from learning from them about how to get a cab. Anger isn't always a bad thing, sometimes it can help you to get out of the rain. Some people never smile, even when they are happy, but you can always learn something from everyone. You can always pay someone to help you with things you don't know, but sometimes it's better to save the $5 for a Strawberry Chocolate Dip Blizzard.

You don't always have to figure it out, but you do have to raise your hand and ask for what you want. When you don't get what you want, there are at least 12,000 other opportunities around the corner. You simply can't be afraid of the word "no." In fact, "no" can be one of your most powerful words.

Chapter Four

Guilt

"Only an unconscious person tries to manipulate, but then only an unconscious person can be manipulated."

Eckhart Tolle

At some point on your journey of re-invention you get tired. You feel like you are paddling upstream. You're tired of living your life for everyone else. You are tired of feeling guilty. When you get tired of being tired, you get angry.

The anger is a sign you are ready to start living with more authenticity. You are willing to stop giving up part of yourself to please everyone else.

Before your journey of re-invention, you did things you didn't really want to do. Or you believed that by doing these things you didn't want to do, you would in some way attract success. You believed that if you did favors, others would notice and you might get an opportunity. When others failed to pay the favor back, you felt resentful. Your resentment turned to anger. Then you felt guilty for feeling angry.

When you do things you have no passion for, be aware of your hidden agenda. Ask yourself if you are secretly trying to manipulate, gain approval, get the spotlight, or avoid the "guilt-trip trap."

If you want to reach your potential, you must learn to take responsibility for all of your decisions. You know that you have learned this lesson when you begin to do things because they benefit you, you desire to do them, you are inspired by them or simply because you want to. No more and no less.

The Power of "No"

Nothing creates more anxiety than doing something you don't want to do simply because you are trying to get rid of the guilt of saying "no". After surveying over 200 women, the results are in. Women juggle way too many responsibilities, wish they had more time for themselves, want more balance and still feel guilty for all the things they aren't getting done. Yet, these same women continue to make commitments to things for which they feel very little energy or passion.

In seminars or in self-help books, the answer is easy; just say, "No." However, in real life most women avoid the "n" word like the plague. Most women would rather feel guilt than disappoint someone or confront someone that won't take "no" for an answer. I call this getting sucked into the "guilt-trip trap."

> The "guilt trip" is that little mental vacation of negative self-talk you take right before you get manipulated into saying "yes" when you'd rather say "no."

The distinction between the "guilt trip" and the "guilt-trip trap" is microscopic, but important. The "guilt trip" is that little mental vacation of negative self-talk that you take right before you get manipulated into saying "yes" when you'd rather say "no." In contrast, the "guilt-trip trap" is when you stick to your guns and say "no", but lose a relationship in the process. Either way you feel like a loser. The manipulator, (those who extend the invitation to the guilt trip) use shame-producing statements in an attempt to force you in to doing what they want, or trapping you into a no-win power struggle so that you learn never to say "no" again.

The manipulator can be your mother, your neighbor, your coworker or your boss. Their success with tripping or trapping you is dependent upon the power they hold over you, your need for their approval. The invitation to take the guilt trip can take the form of a question or a statement or a combination of both. The reason we get tricked or trapped is because most us don't recognize "the invitation" until we have already packed our bags and jumped on the guilt train.

> The challenge with saying "no" and sticking to your guns is you have to quit hoping the other person will agree or understand.

I have known highly successful, grown women who simply couldn't say "no" to their mother because their mother was so good at inviting them to the guilt trip. When mom says something like, "You mean I went through 24 hours of painstaking labor just to give birth to you, and you can't spend 15 minutes more on the phone with me?" The same woman, who was dying to end a phone conversation, packs her bags and stays for an extended visit on the phone to alleviate the guilt that has just been triggered.

For some women, it's their coworkers who are the masters at the invitation. The manipulating coworker says things like, "I have two kids and a husband to take care of, and here you are, single, with no obligations. It won't hurt you to do your fair share and chair the committee this year." Because you see the small kernel of truth in their statement, you go ahead and accept the invitation and comply with their request, even though you feel guilty for not being true to yourself.

Or maybe it's your multitalented, single neighbor who does the inviting. You get asked to head up the neighborhood barbeque and when you say "no," the invitation to the guilt trip goes something like this: "Well, I always get stuck with it. I'm a single woman who has to mow my yard, pay all of my own bills and work full time. At least you have another income and your son mows the yard. Would it hurt you to help out just this one time?"

Five Levels of the Guilt-Trip Trap

Although this kind of statement makes you boil inside, once again you see the logic and you go ahead with the request. By now you've probably noticed a pattern, but if you want to avoid the guilt-trip trap you must know about the five levels of consciousness and the stages you will go through before learning to give a clean clear "no."

Level 1 is when you say "yes" when you want to say "no" simply because you don't want to be judged as one who doesn't pull her fair share, and because you want to avoid the invitation all together. The outcome is that you feel taken advantage of and you feel guilty about not being true to yourself.

At Level 2, you are able to say "no" but then you get pressured (invited to the guilt trip), so you change your answer to "yes" to alleviate the guilt. Initially you feel good because you avoided conflict, but when the time comes to fulfill your commitment, you seethe with resentment toward the person who pressured you. You try to avoid that person so you don't get tricked into saying "yes" again.

> The "Guilt-Trip Trap" is when you stick to your guns and say "no", but lose a relationship in the process.

Internal conflict is the benchmark of Level 3. Level 3 is when you say "yes," but know deep down inside that you aren't going to comply. At Level 3, you are just trying to cope. You are confused by your commitment to be true to yourself and to make sure you don't make someone else mad. You compensate for your confusion by making up a last-minute excuse, like being sick or having a wreck, so you can wiggle out of the commitment. If you are truly conflicted, you actually do get sick and it becomes a pattern to the point of others viewing you as undependable. When you get sick, it's just your internal guidance system paying you back for betraying yourself.

The worst part of Level 3 is you feel guilty for lying, and you feel weak for not having the guts to stand up for yourself. Most of us waver between Levels 1, 2 and 3, depending upon the circumstances and the dynamics of the relationship. Very few of us get to Level 4 or Level 5. We are scared to death of Level 4 because that is the angry, take-no-prisoners level.

The one good thing about Level 4 is there is no more confusion. You are clear that you can and will set the boundary, be it your mother, your coworker, your neighbor or your boss. You are able to say "no" and you are willing to shout it loud and clear should anyone misunderstand. The problem with Level 4 is that the pendulum has swung too far to the right. The anger that gives you the courage to voice your own boundaries is also the unmanageable force that threatens the relationships you worked so hard to build.

At Level 4, you are primed for the invitation and you are determined not to let yourself get sucked into the invitation to the guilt trip. At Level 4, you are good at identifying the invitation, however, the anger you feel from actually noticing the manipulation is enough to momentarily make you lose consciousness. So when your manipulator says something like, "I have already spent two weeks on this project and I've had to deal with blah, blah, blah, and the least you could do is blah, blah, blah," your response is as spontaneous as a volcano, "Well then, you win the crown, the scepter and the robe!"

Immediately you feel a surge of power instead of the guilt you have become so used to. You have successfully traded guilt for anger. Then when the lava begins to cool down, you realize it is the guilt-trip trap that you were so afraid of to begin with.

The manipulator is mad because the manipulation didn't work, and you are mad because she won't listen to your boundary. Even though you feel justified by sticking to your guns, you are preoccupied with the conversation that just took place. You spend your time obsessing about it, trying to convince yourself that you really don't care and that you had every right to blow up. The only problem is that you do care, and now you have an even bigger mess to clean up.

There is a way to Stop Your Drama™ so that you don't get sucked into the Guilt-Trip Trap. All you have to do is say a clear, clean "no." No excuses, no justifications, no explaining, whining, comparing or power struggles. The challenge is that you have to quit hoping the other person will agree or understand.

When you notice the invitation (you are reminded about your mother's labor pains, or your single friend's dilemma of mowing her own yard, or your married friend's problems of having too many responsibilities, and so on), let the initial waves of guilt wash over you. Then you can smile and say, "I'm sorry," and let go of your need for their approval.

Or if you need to extend the dialogue, you can say any combination of the following: "Yes, I see your point of view. I don't know how you do it. I hope you will respect my answer. I hate to disappoint you, but I would hate more to disappoint myself."

Then even if they do stomp off angry, remind yourself that you don't have to play tit-for-tat. You are big enough to handle their anger and to forgive them for the error of their ways.

> Even if they do stomp off angry, remind yourself that you don't have to play tit-for-tat.

SIGNPOSTS

1. You let go of the fantasy that others need to understand your reasons.

2. Your survival is not dependent upon the approval of others.

3. It is okay to like people who are angry with you.

4. It is now easy to see the trap before it is set.

5. You have a new respect for others' right to say "no."

6. You quit believing that it can't get done without you.

7. You quit doing things just to keep the peace.

8. Your own opinion of you matters more than other people's opinion of you.

9. There is more free time to do what you really want.

Getting comfortable with the word "no" means you are coming into your own power. You know how to set boundaries and you are okay if others don't understand your reasons. You have more time to do the things you really want to do, and your friendships are authentic and based on mutual respect instead of codependency.

When you get comfortable with your own anger and you ability to say "no," it's because you are learning to trust yourself, and you now have the courage to ask for what you want because you are no longer afraid of the answer. You know you'll get what you want one way or another.

CHAPTER FIVE

Courage

"Ask and it shall be given you."

Matthew 7:7

Before you started re-inventing your life, you took on more than you needed to and you spent much of your time anticipating the needs of everyone else. Your intuitive skills were so fine-tuned that even a sigh of discomfort from your spouse had you rushing to lend a hand.

You have always anticipated when someone in your family needs help, and you jumped in without them having to ask. That's why you feel frustrated that no one seems to notice when you sigh heavily and could use a helping hand. No one ever picks up on your subtle clues or hints that you need assistance, or that you need to work without interruption, find someone's socks, figure out what's for dinner or referee an argument.

You absolutely resent the idea that you should have to ask for any of your needs to be met. This is especially true if you are trying to start a home-based business and you are having a difficult time with the boundaries of home versus business. For one thing, even if you see yourself as a business owner, your family still

> Develop the courage to do what most people will not do: Ask for what you want.

sees you as wife or mom and does not respect what it takes for you to re-invent yourself. This is extremely frustrating to move forward when your environment is not supportive of your new dreams.

Frustration is a Sign

Your resentment and frustration are signs that you need to make a change. The change is to develop the courage to do what most people will not do: Ask for what you want.

Most people ignore this sign, and instead believe frustration is a signal that someone else needs to change. This is not true. Since you are the one who is unhappy, it is your problem and it is up to you to change. Ignoring the sign of frustration is a safe way to justify your resentment and avoid the risk of rejection that comes from courageously asking.

The fear of rejection is one reason most people won't ask for what they want. A second reason is no one wants to appear vulnerable or stupid as can be seen in this fact: Men don't like to ask for directions and women don't like to ask for help around the house. The man doesn't want to look stupid, and the woman doesn't want to have her request rejected.

Most likely, if a man had the courage to ask for directions, he would get from Point A to Point B much quicker and save some gas. If the woman had the courage to ask for help around the house, she could enjoy some time with her family instead of resenting everyone else while she cleans up after them.

Refusal to Ask is a Sign of Pride

Besides the fear of rejection or the risk of looking stupid, the refusal to ask is really a sign that your pride needs to be tamed. Men and women pay a high price to keep pride in tact. The price is stress and anger toward those who can't read our minds. Refusing to ask means we can make the other people wrong and we can feel superior, and this happens in subtle ways every day.

On several occasions I have watched someone walking behind a slowpoke at a mall or grocery store, and the clueless slowpoke meanders mid-aisle, blocking access to pass through. Maybe I notice this because it's my husband's pet peeve to be slowed down by a clueless, traffic-blocking slowpoke.

The sluggard is in his own world, oblivious to the mounting aggravation or blocked traffic behind him, i.e., my husband, who is now hinting at the frustration by sighing, eye rolling, and throat clearing. Of course from my perspective, it's entertaining to observe. Since I see it coming, I instinctively laugh at what is so obviously funny to me: All it would take is a simple, "Excuse me, would you let me through," and most likely Clueless Clem would saunter over to the side to let us pass. Neither my husband nor I make the request, so we suffer in silence. In fact, we are the only ones feeling any pain.

The other choice is just to slow down and wait until the path is clear, but instead we always get irritated and discuss how other people are clueless. Overall I think all people are about the same in their resistance to asking.

If you were a fly on the wall, you might witness a woman silently fuming while loading the dishwasher without any help wishing her partner would just notice and offer a helping hand. When women get together with their friends, you will invariably hear someone say, "Why do I always have to ask for everything?"

Occasionally you remind yourself that while there would be some obvious advantages of having others read your mind, you wouldn't want to give up your private thoughts for that advantage.

Asking Requires Courage

Asking always involves some measure of risk; however, the willingness to risk asking for what you want means that you are becoming more responsible. Asking for what you want is a sign of confidence and courage. Yet, as I write this, I remember very plainly how not wanting to ask almost had me stranded in the wilderness, a high price to pay for keeping pride in tact. The story takes place at Winter Park, Colorado, after a full day of skiing with my husband.

We ended up on the other side of the mountain near the end of the day. The temperature was falling, and the ice that had formed on my husband's beard made me think of stories about people getting stranded in the wilderness after some plane crash or some mountain climbing expedition. I envisioned how difficult it would be to spend even one night in this wilderness without warmth, food or shelter. I prayed a quick prayer of thanksgiving as I anticipated getting back to the condo for a hot shower, a good meal and a comfortable bed.

Even though there was still one hour left of slope time, I was exhausted from skiing down a blue slope that had me tumbling and falling for the last half of the ride down. Knowing that I didn't have the strength to go up the mountain again, I pleaded my case. "I'm exhausted. Let's just walk to the base of the mountain. Surely we are near the bottom section of the park and can get there from here," I reasoned. After I ignored my husband's recommendation that we ski over to another lift and work our way down, reluctantly my husband agreed that it might be possible to get to the bottom of the mountain from where we stood.

Rather than taking the time to figure out where we needed to go exactly, we made several assumptions and took off walking toward a nearby parking lot where people were putting their skis on their racks and getting ready to head home. At that point, I wished we had brought our SUV instead of taking the bus. Here we were, looking

> Sticky situations always trigger your "stuff."

for the base of the mountain and realizing that we were nowhere near the shuttle stop that would take us out of Winter Park.

My husband and I kept trudging on as if we knew where we were going, and I blindly followed his lead, even though my gut told me that we were headed in the wrong direction.

Finally, as we were almost out of the parking lot area, we hollered at a man who was getting ready to leave, "How do we get to the base of the mountain?"

The man yelled back, "Just go up that hill and it will take you there."

Now, going up a hill did not seem like the way to get down to the base, but without questioning him, the two of us took off like chickens with our heads cut off. Before long we were walking up a snowy hill on a deserted road with no sign of civilization. My shins ached with each step and the weight of carrying my skis on my shoulders made me wish I had taken up snowboarding instead. Not my idea of an enjoyable vacation.

Anyone who has ever been skiing understands this kind of pain. The boots are stiff and heavy, and walking up a snowy hill hauling a pair of skis on your back is anything but fun or comfortable. Fears started to creep in as I visualized us spending the night on a deserted road in the middle of Winter Park in subzero weather, with not so much as a tent or sleeping bag.

"Are you sure we are headed in the right direction?" I asked my husband.

"I guess," was his reply.

"I hate guessing," was my response.

"I can't carry you," was his retort.

The drama was beginning to brew. Sticky situations always trigger your "stuff," and one of mine is getting lost or not knowing my way. I suppose my husband may have the issue more common to men, shouldering the burden or being expected to always have the right answer.

We had a few cross words and I felt like a victim. I saw no choices in the situation. Anger and resentment surfaced. It felt to me like my husband was angry with me for not being willing to get on a lift and ski back down, so as punishment he had decided to "guess" rather than take an active role in getting us back down. At the same time, rather than taking joint responsibility for getting us back to the park, I just wanted him to fix it.

Sometimes it just seems easier to make someone else responsible. If the other person would just figure it out or do something differently, then everything would work out. This kind of expectation puts a heavy burden on any relationship, yet it happens all the time in marriages.

I started praying for an answer. I prayed to let go of judgment. I prayed to accept this present moment, and I also prayed for an angel to guide us to the right place.

Prayer Answered

Barreling down the winding, snowy road came a man driving a huge Ford SUV. Recognizing this as a possible answer to my prayer, I flagged the SUV down.

He came to a stop and rolled down his window.

"We need to get back to Winter Park," I said.

"Just go that way about half a mile and you can even ski there," he said, pointing down the slope of the hill that we had just climbed.

My frustration mounted and I felt like screaming. My gut was right; we were going in the wrong direction all along! At the time I did not recognize the frustration as a sign of needing to ask for what I wanted. Instead I kept thinking someone else needed to change things for me.

"We just came from there," I shrieked, hoping he would somehow sense my frustration, read my mind and offer us a ride back to our condo. The driver didn't sense what I was hinting around to.

When You Ask, You Get

Thinking quickly before the opportunity passed, I said, "Here's the truth: What we really need is to get back to our condo. I am exhausted. We have gotten lost, and I simply can't go any further without some help."

"Hop in the truck," he said, "I'll just take you there."

Prayer answered.

As I climbed into the back of his SUV, I realized a powerful point: You have to ask for what you really want, and you need to be careful what you ask for because you will never get more than you asked for.

SIGNPOSTS ▶

1. You quit expecting others to have your answers.

2. You no longer blame others for the outcomes of your life.

3. You don't expect others to read your mind.

4. You no longer view "asking" as a weakness.

5. Clarity comes.

6. It becomes easier to tell the truth about what you really want.

7. You are willing to risk hearing "no."

8. You know you'll get what you want anyway.

So much of the time we hint, or we expect others to read our minds. You can ask all the questions in the world, but if your request isn't clear, you won't get what you really want. You will be frustrated and resentful that you don't get what you want, when in reality you just don't know how to ask. Once there is clarity in your request, you have done your part. The answer is always "no" until you ask.

If you are really clear about what you want, you'll get it one way or another. Whether you get the answer you want or not, asking is about the willingness to win big.

Chapter Six

Winning

"There is one quality that one must possess to win, and that is the definiteness of purpose, the knowledge of what one wants and a burning desire to possess it."

Napoleon Hill

As you re-invent your life, you look back on your former successes and you see places where you missed the boat. You have been playing not to lose rather than playing to win. You want the second half of life to be different. You see the big picture, take more risks, and ask for what you want.

Staying for over 20 years in a job that you don't like is playing not to lose rather than playing to win. Ignoring your relationship problems is playing not to lose rather than playing to win. Conserving money rather than investing in your education is playing not to lose rather than playing to win.

When you re-invent your life, your ideas about winning change. You realize you aren't competing against anyone but yourself. Stephen Covey, in his book, *The Seven Habits of Highly Effective People*, says, "Private victories precede public victories." For example, it used to feel like winning if I could prove my point in an argument. Now it's more of a win if I can be patient, listen, ask questions and have a new understanding.

> If you want to know what someone's life philosophy for winning is, all you have to do is observe.

Winning little is about competition. Winning big is about collaborating. In order to win big, you must conquer many personal challenges to develop character qualities such as patience, self-discipline and self-reflection.

You can tell a lot about a person by their philosophy about winning, for example, coach Vince Lombardi said, "Winning isn't everything, it's the only thing," while tennis pro Arthur Ashe said, "You've got to get to the stage in life where going for it is more important than winning or losing." Donald Trump might say that in business, it's all about the bottom line. If Mother Theresa were alive, she might say that winning is about giving love.

The Signs of Your Philosophy

You also have a philosophy about winning whether you know it or not, and whether you give voice to your philosophy. Your winning philosophy shows up in the choices you make every day. If you want to know what someone's life philosophy for winning is, all you have to do is observe and look for the signs. Learning how to read the signs helps you determine a lot about a person's character. This skill comes in handy no matter what your endeavors. This story about a restaurant experience illustrates the point.

A couple of my friends and I decided to try a new restaurant. I was excited to see that the restaurant offered a variety of salads. What makes a salad good, in my opinion, is the various kinds of dark green leaves. After looking at the menu and deciding on a particular salad, I asked the waitress, "Are your salads made with iceberg lettuce, or do you mix in some dark lettuce such as romaine or field greens?"

"We use iceberg," she answered.

Showing visible disappointment, I made a request. "I'd like to have some dark lettuce added if you don't mind." (See, I was learning to ask for what I wanted.) The waitress informed me that the lettuce the restaurant purchased came in big bags premixed and does not come with any dark green lettuce, and is simply a mixture of iceberg, carrots and red cabbage. "No problem," I thought to myself. I had noticed the restaurant offered a Caesar salad on the menu and I knew that Caesar salads are made with romaine. My idea of winning in this particular instance was to get the kind of salad I wanted by making a few adjustments to the lettuce that was offered. It seemed like a win-win deal to me.

> Any time you do not step up to the plate, you have just sacrificed the big contest to win the little one.

"I noticed you have Caesar salad on the menu, and it is made with romaine lettuce," I said, hoping the waitress would see the logic of adding some romaine to the salad I wanted. Instead she made another suggestion. "Yes, we do have Caesar salad. Would you rather order a Caesar salad instead?" My first reaction was that I had not completely and clearly asked for what I really wanted. What I really wanted was the kind of salad I think is good. It was apparent that the waitress had not considered how to be creative. However, as person who is dedicated to developing others, I saw a prime opportunity to teach her Problem Solving 101. "I have an idea," I said to her. "Would you mind tearing off a couple leaves of romaine and adding that to the salad I want to order instead of making me order a salad I don't really want?"

She paused for a moment, placed her hand on her hip and said,

"We are extremely busy right now and I don't think the cook would appreciate me making more work for him." I was stunned at her answer, which is so contrary to customer service that I wanted to check my perception.

"So, it's not about customer service, but it is about keeping the cook happy?" I responded out of shock. My statement didn't rattle her in the least.

"No, it's not that I don't want to give you what you want," she said, "Hey, I would tear and wash the lettuce myself if I wasn't so busy."

It was obvious to me that for the waitress, winning meant making the cook happy, or getting out of work, or making excuses rather than solving the problem.

The problem with this kind of philosophy is that the little contest is won but the big contest is lost. The big contest is seeing the big picture. Sure, the cook might grumble or feel a bit of a time crunch. Sure, the waitress might be busy, but isn't the real win all about serving the customer so that the customer comes back and brings friends, and spends money in the restaurant? I'm fairly certain that the owner of the restaurant views winning more from the customer's point of view.

Winning Little versus Winning Big

We human beings often sacrifice the big contest to win the little one. When you work to make it easy on yourself, you win the little contest but you lose the big contest of winning the customer over. When you argue with your spouse and you win, you only win the little contest. The big contest is making the commitment to the relationship. When you resort to sarcasm, cheat on a test, skip your workout, make excuses, blame other people, show poor sportsmanship, or any time you do not step up to the plate, you have just sacrificed the big contest to win the little one.

Many years ago I competed in the sport of competitive bodybuilding. Bodybuilding is an unusual sport. You work out for hours every day, stay on a strict diet for months to shed as much fat as possible. You learn the mandatory poses, and from those poses you develop a routine that you perform to music to showcase the muscles you have worked so hard to develop.

Several times I won state contests and this enabled me to go to nationals twice. I placed 10th in California and I placed 13th in Texas. This doesn't sound so bad at a national contest where you are competing against 50 other competitors, however, unless you place in the top five, you are not allowed to do your posing routine on the evening of the contest. All of those hours of pumping iron and suffering through the diet, and you don't get to do the routine. The routine is the only fun part of bodybuilding as far as I was concerned. It wasn't the winning that I cared about. On a national level, I didn't really care if I placed first or 10th. The routine was where I shined and it was a third of the final score if you could make it to the top five. Nonetheless, the opportunity to showcase the routine eluded me two times.

> Winning big requires self-discipline to follow through even though you want to quit. The big contest is about stepping up on the stage just because the invitation is there to do so.

However, each time at nationals, there was an option for each competitor to go ahead and suit up and be introduced and strike a pose or two. That meant staying on the diet another 12 hours or so. (After all, it would be embarrassing to be smoothed out and bloated while being introduced against the top national competitors.) Since suiting up wasn't required, both times I opted out. Why bother? I wasn't bitter, just disappointed and it didn't seem logical to be on stage when it wouldn't matter in the long run. Once the option to pose was no longer available, all I could think about was Mexican food. A big enchilada awaited me, and it had been four months since I'd had a fattening meal.

Looking back, I realize that both times I was looking to win the little contest and I sacrificed the big contest. The little contest is getting the applause for the posing routine. The little contest is placing in the top five, getting the trophy, and beating the other competitors. The little contest is about calling it quits and going for the enchilada. No matter how many times you win the little contests in life, it is important to remember that there is always a bigger contest to be won.

> You win big when you follow through even though you want to quit.

Self-Discipline is a Sign

Self-discipline is one of the signs of winning big. You win big when you follow through even though you want to quit. Another sign of winning big is the decision to be happy for other competitors who paid their dues and placed in the top five. Winning big is about making a choice that stretches you just because the opportunity presents itself. Winning big is about stepping up on the stage just because the invitation is there to do so.

Two times I had the opportunity, but I failed to see the big contest because my focus was on the little contest. That choice to suit up, diet another 12 hours and take the stage would have defined me like an enchilada never could.

Seeing the big picture moves you to the next level and is just as important for a waitress, a factory worker, a boss, a motivational speaker, a spouse, a football coach and a business owner.

SIGNPOSTS ▶

1. It becomes easy to distinuish the little contest from the big contest.

2. It's never a loss if a lesson was learned.

3. You start building a life philosophy.

4. Self-discipline becomes a way of life.

5. You appreciate opportunities that stretch you.

6. Your choices define you.

Winning big is about seeing the big picture and consciously making choices that move you to be the kind of person you are capable of being. Your conscious choices define you, but your unconscious actions give the world a glimpse into your real world, your relationship with yourself.

Chapter Seven

Self Love

"Betrayal of yourself in order not to betray another is betrayal nonetheless. It is the highest betrayal."

Neale Donald Walsch

At various times on your success journey others disappoint you. There's a part of you that tries to get security and validation from others, and your expectations become distorted. You believe that if your spouse would just appreciate you, or if your kids would just behave, if your boss would see your value, or if you just lived in a different area, things would be different. It seems that what you do is never good enough. You are searching for a kind of love that cannot be found from the outside, and the more you demand that others appreciate you, the more you lose your power to what others think, say or do.

Your Gift to Yourself

A sign of your transformation is when you realize that you can't get from others what you don't give to yourself. You cannot find love without first loving and trusting yourself, for you cannot betray yourself and find love.

For all the discussion and confusion on what love is and is not, it has become clear that loving yourself, trusting yourself and having high self-esteem are all related.

One way you show love for yourself is by treating yourself right. When you act in your best interests, your self-esteem is high because you have learned to trust yourself. Trusting yourself is linked to the number of times you consistently act in your own best interests. When you let others run over you, hurt you, or make decisions that are not in your best interests, you betray yourself and your self-esteem plummets. Yet sometimes we sacrifice ourselves in an effort to be humble, or to avoid conflict. We simply trade the external conflict for the internal conflict.

William Shakespeare said, "Self-love, my liege, is not so vile a sin, as self-neglecting." Okay, let me translate what Shakespeare meant: It's okay to love yourself. In fact, the sin is in neglecting yourself, yet how often do we give up a piece of ourselves just to please other people? Neale Donald Walsch says in Book Number 2 of Conversations With God, "Betrayal of yourself in order not to betray another is betrayal nonetheless. It is of the highest betrayal."

When you speak up when someone has done you wrong, you learn to trust that you will take care of yourself. When you hold others accountable for their actions and learn to make decisions that work in your best interests, then you build a solid foundation of trust for yourself. Without this foundation, it is easy to crumble when the going gets tough.

> When you have a high level of trust for yourself, you make your decisions based on who you are, not on what other people will or will not do.

Give Generously to Yourself

Loving and trusting yourself is the foundation for building relationships with others. You can only honor others to the degree that you honor yourself, and you can only trust others when you have learned to trust yourself. Sometimes we get confused about the order and priority of loving ourselves versus loving others, and the result is often the betrayal of self.

Sarah and Nathan, friends of mine, went through a painful divorce which resulted in foreclosure, bankruptcy and Sarah becoming a single parent of four children. Throughout their 20+ years of marriage, Nathan had a habit of breaking promises to Sarah, yet she turned a blind eye to all of Nathan's faults and never confronted Nathan about his behaviors. Sarah would always say, "I love him for better and for worse."

> Letting others make all of your decisions is a sign that you do not trust yourself.

Denial is a Sign

Denial is a sign that you do not trust yourself enough to handle the truth. Sarah denied looking at Nathan's behaviors and justified her denial so she could hold on to the marriage. Facing the truth would have required Sarah to confront Nathan, leave him, or demand significant changes. If Sarah would have had the courage to face the truth, the indicators would have been easy to spot.

Why should an intelligent woman trust a man who has betrayed her on every level? These things were not hidden from Sarah, yet she failed to hold Nathan accountable to his role as husband and father. In the process, Sarah learned not to trust herself and slowly lost self-respect.

Letting others make all of your decisions is a sign that you do not trust yourself. Although Nathan's actions were anything but loving, Sarah continued to "love him" at the expense of herself, always deferring to him in major decisions regarding their life. Sarah never learned how to trust herself, and working through a strenuous divorce settlement left her bewildered, confused and lonely.

When Nathan and Sarah were negotiating the divorce settlement, Sarah confessed that she didn't know what she needed in terms of financial assistance to help her to care for their children. Nathan said to Sarah, "You are just going to have to trust me to be fair with you."

Trust Must be Earned

No intelligent woman should trust anyone, man or woman, who proves to be untrustworthy? Trust is not an unconditional gift we give to others. Trust is not turning a blind eye to the facts of the situation or to the history of the past. Trust is based on information, previous experiences, consistency, and past history.

We trust that when the traffic light is green, it means we are clear to go—so we take action upon that trust and we proceed through traffic. We trust when a doctor says, "This won't hurt at all," that we won't experience pain and with that trust we give our permission for the doctor to continue. If, however, a particular traffic light were inconsistent or unreliable, it would be foolish to completely trust that light. You would instead use your judgment first, then you would proceed through the light. The point is this: Trust and love yourself first, then you are free to trust and love others.

> Trust and love yourself first, then you are free to trust and love others.

Trust Yourself First

This thought occurred to me as I was on an airplane on my way to a speaking engagement traveling with my friend, Michele. Michele and I took our seats on the plane and we introduced ourselves to the woman sitting in the aisle seat.

Right before takeoff, the airline attendant pointed out the fact that Michele and I were seated by the emergency exit and the flight attendant asked Michele, who was seated by the window, if she was comfortable with the responsibility of assisting other passengers in the event of an emergency, by kicking out the exit door.

Michele said, "Yes," then laughingly turned to the other woman and me, and said, "Do you two trust me with your life?" Although I knew Michelle was joking, the other woman answered thoughtfully and deliberately,

"No, but I trust me."

I reflected on this conversation several times and realized that when you have a high level of trust for yourself, you won't make your decisions based on what other people will or will not do. You trust yourself enough to know that you will do what is best for yourself. That kind of attitude will take you out of the negative patterns of resentment and blame and it eliminates the possibility of you playing the victim role.

> Loving someone else should never threaten the trust you have for yourself.

Conversely, my friend Sarah in her attempts to be patient, kind and long-suffering all in the name of "love" had betrayed herself. By remaining silent, by accepting

broken promises, she had deceived herself and there-
by learned not to trust herself. Loving someone else
should never threaten the trust you have for yourself.
The truth is you cannot love someone else until you
learn to love yourself. Love doesn't happen at the expense of yourself.

When Sarah's ex-husband uttered the words "trust
me," it occurred to her that what she needed most was
to trust herself, and that trusting herself would be an
outward sign that she did indeed love herself.

One of my favorite authors, Gary Zukav, says that
when you present yourself a doormat, others will clean
their shoes on you. Nathan had been cleaning his shoes
on Sarah for more than twenty years because she did
not have the courage to challenge him. In failing to
make Nathan accountable for his role of husband and
father, Sarah betrayed herself.

Developing trust for yourself is one way you show
love for yourself. You learn to trust yourself when you
love yourself enough to set a boundary in an unhealthy
relationship or when you demand a higher standard as
to how you intend to be treated. You show respect and
trust for yourself when you ask for what you want and
know that you are strong enough to face the outcome.
You love yourself when you are vulnerable enough to

share your feelings and yet strong enough to face the risk of rejection.

Important relationships dissolve, couples break up and romance ends. There is one relationship that you can't escape, and that is the one you have with yourself. Of all the people who will ever come into your life, YOU are the only one you will never leave; therefore you deserve your love and attention as much as anyone else does.

> There is one relationship that you can't escape, and that is the one you have with yourself.

SIGNPOSTS ▶

1. Integrity in relationships is more important than people pleasing.

2. Trusting yourself is a way you build integrity with yourself.

3. Others are held to a higher standard because of your high standards.

4. You give love but not at the expense of yourself.

5. Boundaries are clear and easily communicated.

6. You become your own best friend.

7. You quit hanging out with people who do not respect you.

Before you can really love and give to others, you must love and give to yourself. Even the airline attendants will tell you to put on your own oxygen mask first before helping someone else with theirs. When you give up part of yourself to please others, you betray yourself and learn not to trust you.

Shakespeare said, "This above all: To thine own self be true, and it must follow, as the night the day, thou canst not then be false to any man." Was he talking about love?

Chapter Eight

Worthiness

"Simply making consistent investments in our self-education and knowledge banks pays major dividends throughout our lives."

Jim Rohn

If you study anyone who is at the top of her game, you will find someone who has not only paid her dues, but someone who invests heavily in herself. You've probably heard the old saying "You can tell what someone's priorities are by looking at their checkbook and the way they spend their time." Investing in yourself is a sign of self-worth.

When you view yourself as important and worthy, you invest in yourself and you don't let anyone determine your own personal or professional growth. You don't go around making excuses as to why you can't attend a conference or you can't purchase a self-study course. You'll pay for it if you see fit. Entrepreneurs invest in themselves all the time, however, many people who work as an employee have not yet developed the awareness that they are responsible for their own advancement.

When you invest in something, you expect to see a return. You want a richer career, more knowledge, the capacity to earn more money, or a healthier body. When you invest in something, it is because you believe there is value and worth in the investment. That is why you also invest in the health of your body.

> You can tell a lot about a person's level of self-worth consciousness by the way she spends her time and her money.

I can hardly believe my ears when I hear people say, "I haven't been to the doctor in years because it's so expensive." My response is, "Dying isn't cheap either." Why do we seem to undervalue things, which are irreplaceable and overvalue things that can be easily replaced?

Most of us don't invest the proper amount of time or money to maintain our health, yet we think nothing of spending money on cars, boats, and entertainment systems which, although quite expensive, can be replaced. The same people who won't spend $50 on a massage, a manicure or a spa treatment wouldn't think twice about spending $50 on an automobile for an oil change, not to mention unconsciously spending the same amount at the vending machines over the course of a month.

Neglect of Health is a Sign

When you won't invest in your own health, it's an indication of low self-esteem and a low value of self-worth. Years ago I referred a business associate, Jessica, to a massage therapist to help her with some health challenges. After several massages, Jessica marveled about the health benefits she was receiving. "I'm feeling more optimistic, I'm not missing work anymore and I so look forward to the treatment," she declared. Then Jessica said something that indicated her level of consciousness regarding her health: "As much as I love the benefits, I don't know how I can continue to justify spending $50 a month on a massage."

It was almost as if Jessica was screaming to the world, "I'm not worth it!" The fact is, nothing is more important than your health and there is no need to justify spending $50 to keep your body in working order.

Ask a person with cancer or Parkinson's disease what they would give up to have their health. Then compare that with the relatively healthy person who needs to justify a decision to purchase vitamins or get a massage. You never need to justify your worth.

Just because you were born is evidence enough that you deserve to be here. However, at Jessica's request, I came up with 10 "justifications" for a massage:

1. You are feeling optimistic.

2. You look forward to the treatment.

3. You haven't missed a day of work since you started the massage.

4. It benefits your health.

5. You enjoy the massage therapist.

6. It's a nice way to reward yourself.

7. It's a better vice than smoking cigarettes.

8. It's a way to care for yourself.

9. It improves circulation and flexibility.

10. You are worth it.

Of course it doesn't matter what my opinion is regarding Jessica's decision to get or not get a massage.

The decision is not mine to make. The only way Jessica will feel good about investing in herself is if she decides she's worth it.

If you continually communicate to yourself and others that you are not worth it, then you are sure to attract people into your life who agree with your philosophy and who will treat you as such. You communicate to yourself that you are worth it by your actions; for example, the way you invest your time and money.

> If you continually communicate to yourself and others that you are not worth it, then you are sure to attract people into your life who agree with your philosophy and who will treat you as such.

So many people deny themselves opportunities because they think it is up to others to tell them that they are worth it. For example, "I'd love to join your association, but my company won't pay for it," or "I'd love to attend that seminar, but my company won't pay for it."

The biggest excuse I've ever heard when it comes to self-growth is, "I can't afford it," or "My boss won't pay for it." When you are committed to re-inventing yourself, you find the way.

A good sign that you are "transforming" is that you don't wait for your company to tell you what kind of association you can belong to or what kind of educational event you can attend, and you don't fall for the belief that you can't afford it. You start to realize that much of the time those statements are nothing more than lazy habits or a lack of real commitment.

Many things are expensive; however, it's a matter of priority. If you want to get a manicure once a week, you might have to give up daily visits to the vending machine.

Lack of time is the second biggest excuse people give for lack of personal growth. "I would love to go to college but I don't have the time." The victim blames time. Responsible, successful people make choices.

If you want to get into shape, you realize that you might have to give up two hours of television. You can usually have the essence of what you want if you are willing to take full responsibility to get it and if you feel that you are worth it. The way you spend time and money are signs

> The way you spend time and money are signs that indicate your level of self-worth consciousness.

that indicate your level of self-worth consciousness, and there are four levels.

The Four Levels of Self-Worth Consciousness

Level 1 is the person who won't invest time or money to get what would make their life better, be it education, health, financial prosperity, or career advancement. These people simply aren't interested. They believe in luck and circumstances more than responsibility and action. These people make excuses about their heredity, their background, their lack of education or anything else that they believe keeps them from reaching success. They believe in everything except themselves. The Level 1 person struggles in his professional career, but won't spend a dime getting coaching, nor will she invest a few hours reading a book that might offer some answers. The Level 1 person needs more time because of balancing a full-time career with raising children, but wouldn't dream of paying for a housekeeper to help her lighten the load. The Level 1 person is capable but frustrated.

Level 2 people are a bit more advanced. The person at Level 2 takes advantage of some opportunities as long as it doesn't stretch him out of his comfort zone. For example, the Level 2 people will gladly go to a workshop or conference if it is on company time and the company pays for it. The Level 2 person is committed to convenience and some learning, however this person would never dream of paying for the knowledge herself. The Level 2 person has never considered purchasing educational books, tapes, or seminars because she does not place a high value on knowledge.

The Level 3 person places a high value on knowledge. In fact, the Level 3 person is the person who continually purchases books and listens to tapes and CDs in his car on a regular basis. This person will invest thousands of dollars attending seminars and workshops; however, the Level 3 person fails to invest the real time it takes to incorporate the learning or the habit. They want to get better, but don't want to or can't find time to put forth the effort. Level 3 people get excited initially, but drop the ball or continue to search for the next "fix" that they believe will help them to the next level.

> In order to meet your needs, you have to believe that you are worth it.

The highest level is Level 4. Level 4 people are willing to invest both their time and their money to grow. These are the people who purchase books and tapes and continue to use them and implement the learning. The Level 4 people are more likely to have an entrepreneurial spirit. If they find value in an organization, they join it even if the company won't pay for it. They feel appreciative if their company pays for their education, but if they have to go to a seminar on their own time to learn a skill, they do so. If they invest the money on education, they will also invest the time it takes to implement. The way a person invests time and money is a mirror of his or her values.

One thing I've noticed about successful people is their understanding that the better they meet their needs, the easier their happiness and success comes. However, in order to meet your needs, you have to believe that you are worth it.

SIGNPOSTS ▶

1. You do good things for yourself.

2. Healthy habits such as exercise and diet are integrated into your life.

3. You communicate to others that you are worthy.

4. When talking about yourself, you say good things.

5. People respect you and relationships flourish.

6. Getting what you want is easy and you are responsible.

7. Personal growth is seen as an investment rather than an expense.

The only things that make your lack of success or lack of worthiness true are your beliefs about success and worthiness. While it's true that sometimes you have to give up one thing to get something else, the real question is, "Am I worth it?" The answer is up to you.

CHAPTER NINE

Power

"As you become more clear about who you really are, you'll be better able to decide what is best for you—the first time around."

Oprah Winfrey

When you get clear about who you are, what you want, and where you are going, you quit seeking approval and start to come into your own power. I used to watch a sitcom, "Malcolm in the Middle" and there was a song that goes, "You're not the boss of me now, you're not the boss of me now, you're not the boss of me now and you're not so big..." This is a good reminder that no one likes to be bossed around, yet so often, we give our power away, even as adults.

We seek our parents' approval for our decisions, even though we are well into our thirties. Or we get married and we ask our spouse's permission instead of acting like an equal partner. It's sometimes valuable to process your thoughts or seek outside opinions, however, no one likes to be told what to do. In fact, a good way to start an argument is to tell someone else what to do. Another way to start an argument is to tell someone that they don't need something that they actually want.

If you've ever heard your spouse tell you that you don't "need" another piece of dessert, another pair of shoes, or a bigger closet, you know what I'm talking about. You may see the kernel of truth in the statement, but it doesn't keep you from wanting the second helping of dessert, the other pair of shoes or the bigger closet, which leads to my next point: There is a vast difference between want and need. You need shelter, but you want the palace; you need clothing, but you want the designer label, and you need transportation, but you want the Cadillac.

> There is a vast difference between want and need.

The Difference Between Want and Need

Nothing good comes from telling someone else what they need, just as nothing good comes from letting others tell you what you need. I learned this lesson when I first got married.

Touché antique store was having a sale. Even with the good discounts, the price tags kept most working class people from entering the store more than once, however it never stopped me from stopping by "just to look." By all appearances, it seemed that those who shop regularly at Touché live in gated communities with four-car garages, double fireplaces on some expansive countryside estate. Nonetheless, as I walked through the store, I found myself daydreaming about the day when I could stop in and purchase what ever I wanted, and there were lots of things that I wanted at Touché.

> Nothing good comes from letting others tell you what you need.

It was the first day of fall when I spotted the mirror, which was displayed over an intricately carved cherry entry table with a marble top. It was the most beautiful mirror I had ever seen, imported from Europe with a thickly hand carved wooden frame of hummingbirds

perched on dogwood branches, washed in hues of salm-
on, sea foam green and amber blending into and out
of the wood making the piece come to life. I reached
over the cherry table and across the massive crystal
bowl of potpourri to grab the price tag, which took my
breath away. Letting go of the tag, I whispered under
my breath, "That's too expensive," and I walked out of
the store, but I didn't forget about the mirror.

Later in the day a thought entered my mind, "Why
not?" Although I had never before even toyed with the
idea of purchasing expensive furniture or artwork, it
was not difficult to answer why I should not purchase
the mirror. Besides the mirror being too expensive, it
seemed logical to believe that factory workers don't buy
things like that, and I was a factory worker. Now there
were two reasons why not.

I also thought about what my husband's response
might be. He might say, "You deserve it, after all, you
work full time and you make your own money." Or he
might say, "You don't need a mirror like that," and it
became my third reason. I couldn't bear the thought
of him denying me my wish so I stayed silent, but I
couldn't get the mirror off my mind.

Later that day during dinner, I decided to tell my
husband about the mirror and I made my opening state-

ments: "Picture if you will, two years from now when we have a new house. In the house we have beautiful furniture and our surroundings are comfortable, yet elegant. In the corner, we have an unusual piece that is admired by everyone. It is a mirror. The mirror is massive, about 3' by 4' and intricately carved by a craftsman in Europe. When people see it they know it is one of a kind. The perfect place for it is over your great-grandmother's antique buffet placed in the entryway." He didn't say anything so I concluded with my closing argument.

"Wouldn't the mirror be something that we would want to keep forever? Wouldn't it be an investment of sorts? It is also something that is very practical, after all it is a mirror and everyone has mirrors in their house, only this one would be special."

> When you fail to recognize your choices, you will feel needy and resentful and you will allow others or your circumstances to make choices for you.

Then he uttered the magic words: "You don't need a mirror like that."

His arguments made perfect sense. We had just married and the house we were living in simply wasn't big enough for a mirror of that size. "There are other things we need right now," he reminded me.

"Someday when we get things lined out, it might be appropriate to start looking for artwork or other unusual pieces, but now is not the time." After thinking twice about the price tag, I could see the logic behind his reasoning.

But...there was something that bothered me. My husband would go to auctions and purchase antique and rusted gas pumps and memorabilia without asking my opinion at all. He would say, "One day I'll restore these and they will be valuable." He viewed these old rusty pumps as an investment, and it didn't bother him to spend lots of money on them even though I

> When you let someone tell you what you want, you rarely get what you need.

did not see value in them. Of course this difference in philosophy caused a bit of conflict in our relationship, as you can imagine.

Even though I was angry at first, my husband was a great teacher for me. When you let someone tell you what you need, you rarely ever get what you want. My husband knew this lesson already. He did not rely on me to tell him what he needed, nor what he wanted.

After much negotiating (well, maybe it was nagging after all,) he must have seen my point of view because he decided that he would go to Touché and surprise me with the mirror for my birthday.

A few days before my birthday, he broke the news. "I know you want that mirror and I tried to buy it for you, but they wouldn't negotiate and give me a good price for it."

Apparently at Touché, they do not respect the word "haggle" and it is considered bad manners to even suggest that the price is "too high." I was able to convince my husband that we should give Touché what they want.

Hubby went back after his haggling attempt and returned to me with some bad news. "I know you were hoping that I would surprise you with the mirror for your birthday, and I was going to even though I was not able to get a good deal on it. When I returned for the purchase, the mirror was no longer there. I don't want you to go into the store and think that I'm going to surprise you, because the mirror is gone. We waited too long."

I was heartbroken, and did not go back into Touché for another year. This "down time" from visiting my favorite antique store helped me to process the situation.

I had given up my own power to let someone else's values determine what was right for me. Letting others make decisions for you is a sign that you do not know how to own your personal power. It was true that I did not need the mirror, but this fact didn't keep me from wanting it. I had given my power to have the mirror to someone else.

Unrecognized Choices

All along there had many choices that I never considered. The mirror could have been put on layaway. It could have been purchased with money from a savings account, or it could have been charged on a credit card. When you fail to recognize your choices, you will feel needy and resentful, and you will allow others or your circumstances to make choices for you. A sign that you are moving to the next level is that you start recognizing your choices. If you don't recognize your choices, you can't make responsible decisions, and as a result, you let others decide for you.

> When you fail to recognize your choices, you will feel needy and resentful, and you will allow others or your circumstances to make choices for you.

About a year later, I went back into Touché to look around and to my surprise the mirror was there. The owner had second thoughts about selling the mirror and took it home to enjoy for a while, and offered the mirror for sale again. This time I purchased the mirror without approval from anyone else. I still have the mirror today, and my husband and I both enjoy the beauty of the mirror.

> To take responsibility for our lives, we have to recognize our choices.

This mirror is a constant reminder to me that to take responsibility for our lives, we have to recognize our choices.

SIGNPOSTS ▶

1. You know the difference between need and want.

2. You respect and consider your desires.

3. Teamwork is important to you.

4. You become clear about your ability to make decisions.

5. You make your own decisions about how to spend your money or time.

6. It's no longer acceptable to control and manipulate others.

7. You ask for opinions, but only for additional information, not advice.

8. You respect other people's desires which may differ from yours.

When a decision can be made without impacting someone else's life, you have to be willing to act in your own best interests to get what you want. When you wait for approval, you discount your power of choice and end up with less than you deserve.

When you let someone else tell you what you need, you rarely ever get what you want. Sometimes you blame others for not supporting you to get what you want, when the only shift you really need is to challenge your outdated beliefs and to let others work through their feelings about your choices.

CHAPTER TEN

Beliefs

"To have doubted one's own first principles is the mark of a civilized man."

Oliver Wendell Holmes

One of the signs of re-invention is when you start questioning everything you once believed. This questioning creates a case of the "crazies." The reason you feel crazy is you have switched positions in the rowboat. Instead of being at the back of the boat following someone else's directions, you are now the captain of your own boat. Your past self found it easier to sit in the back and take direction. Now you are learning to trust yourself and come to your own conclusions about life, relationships, money, and success. You aren't simply taking someone's word for it anymore. Instead of following, you are exploring. You are a seeker.

Rene Descartes said, "If you would be a real seeker after truth, it is necessary that at least once in your life you doubt, as far as possible, all things." It is unsettling to question your beliefs, your religion or your upbringing. You are jumping into the unknown without the only safety net you've ever known, the belief system your parents set up for you as a child.

Beliefs Evolve

It saves energy not to question what you learned as a child. However, the beliefs that work for you as a 5-year–old can become a stumbling block when you are an adult. I'm not talking about the Tooth Fairy or Santa Claus.

Take, for example, the idea that "Children are to be seen and not heard," or the admonition that "Big boys don't cry." As a child, these statements teach you to quit interrupting adults and that it doesn't help you to continue to whine every time you scrape your knee. Your parents did the best they could to raise you to be a responsible adult. However, if you get stuck on how you were raised or adhere to every thing your parents taught you about life, those teachings can make you a puppet rather than an assertive adult. The beliefs that no longer work for you must evolve into beliefs that benefit you as an adult.

I once knew a woman named Linda, a corporate executive at a medical in-stitution, who attracted the most rude and disre-spectful bosses into her life. Linda expressed her

> The beliefs that work for you as a 5-year–old can become a stumbling block when you are an adult.

frustration to me one day over coffee. "He is not as educated as I am, nor does he have my capabilities or experience, yet he is always asking me to clean up his mess, or get him some coffee. He even embarrasses me in front of others at the board meeting."

From all appearances, Linda's boss doesn't respect her. Once you delve a little deeper, it's easy to see that Linda doesn't know how to set boundaries. This inabil-ity comes from her upbringing. When I asked Linda if she had tried to talk with her boss about his bad behav-ior, she said, "No." In Linda's mind, she had no other choices but to quit and look for another job. Remember the previous chapter? As long as you do not see choices you cannot make responsible decisions.

With this idea in mind, I decided to play devil's ad-vocate and it became apparent that Linda was stuck in a pattern. It was out of the question for Linda to confront her boss. There was no way Linda would ask for a meeting with her boss' superior, nor would she make a suggestion to her current boss to hire an assistant to help clean up messes. Linda shunned the idea of experimenting by asking the boss to pick up after her to see what happens. "Maybe he would reciprocate and help you if you just turned the tables," I said to challenge her, but Linda could not see the situation in any other light. Her boss is rude and demanding, end of subject. Linda's frustration should have been a sign to her that she needs to ask for what she wants, but she did not have the courage and she found ways to justify her lack of courage.

"Why don't you just question his motives and tell him you are not available to be his maid?" I finally asked in frustration. Linda's answer was simple and to the point: "That's not how I was raised."

Linda was raised to be subordinate to those in authority. She was not raised to question rude behavior, stand up for her rights or to question a job description. Linda was not raised to own her own power and command respect. It is no doubt that Linda's parents taught her to be respectful and responsible; however, the values that worked for her as a 5-year-old didn't work for her as an adult.

Opinions and Judgments are Signs

A strong opinion or judgment is a good sign that you have a belief that needs to be examined. Otherwise there would be no emotional reaction behind the belief. For example, Shelby, a woman I met at a workshop had adopted her parents' belief that it is wrong to "air out your dirty laundry."

Shelby has strong opinions of people who share too much personal information and she believes it is wrong, because her parents said so. In Shelby's opinion, talk about religion, relationships, or vulnerabilities are off-limits, and people who engage in such topics easily offend her. As you might imagine, Shelby does not have many close relationships.

She is too busy defending her opinions about how everyone else is wrong and she is right. Shelby has never questioned her upbringing. If she did, she might come to a different conclusion. She might conclude that she agrees with the basic philosophy with one or two exceptions, perhaps it is okay to share with a best friend or a significant other. Or perhaps Shelby would conclude that she does agree with the philosophy for herself, but still understand that others are more comfortable sharing personal information. Either way, there wouldn't be the emotional attachment to being right, and Shelby wouldn't believe that her parents were the only ones who knew what they were doing when it comes to raising kids.

If Shelby could challenge her upbringing, she might be able to get closer to others. Instead, she can't get close to anyone because she is so attached to being right that she rarely shares anything about herself. Shelby always comes off as a know-it-all who bases every conversation on the facts and her strong opinions and judgments of what is right and what is wrong. The fear of having her weaknesses used against her is so deeply ingrained

> Challenge your collective agreements by asking the question "Do my agreements work for me or against me?"

that it is safer to believe that mom and dad were right, and that anyone else who has the freedom to share intimate details of their life is wrong for doing so.

Collective Agreements

It's difficult to keep believing something if no one else believes it. On the other hand, it's difficult to challenge a belief if everyone you know believes what you are questioning. Agreement makes belief that much stronger. All of us have agreements with our families, and those agreements turn into unquestioned beliefs that manifest as self-fulfilling prophecies.

Shelby and Linda have made "agreements" with their respective family of origin. Linda agrees with her family that she should never question authority, and Shelby agrees that it is wrong to get up close and personal with anyone. Linda continues to be successful in keeping her agreement not to question authority; however, if Linda wants to experience the success of re-invention, she will have to break her collective agreements.

Shelby is successful keeping people at a distance, but if she wants to experience success in relationships, she may have to shift her collective agreement about not sharing too much information. Success is a given. You just have to determine what kind of success you are committed to.

Sue, a participant in one of my workshops, learned the importance of identifying collective agreements that were keeping her stuck. Her demands about how Christmas "should" be prevented her from seeing new opportunities to become a creator. Sue had a collective agreement about how Christmas "should" be. Christmas should be fun for everyone, and in order for it to be fulfilling, others must appreciate the tree, and others must want to spend time decorating it. For Sue, the holidays continued to be a disappointment because her two teenage boys and husband didn't give a lick about a tree or putting up decorations. This was a huge disappointment to Sue. She always dreaded the holidays because she put so much effort into the things she enjoyed, things others in her family didn't appreciate. Sue's feeling of success regarding Christmas was directly related to things over which she had no control.

Challenging Collective Agreements

With some brainstorming, Sue and I came up with some ways to challenge her collective agreements with her family. One possibility was for Sue to experiment for one year by choosing not to decorate or put together a tree. Then Sue could see what kind of reaction the men of the family really would have. Sue might discover the truth of the matter is that it is okay for her family to act indifferent, as long as there is no threat of losing what they currently have. Sue's other choices included changing her demands of what others need to feel, and focus only on her own wishes.

> Once you develop the power of listening, you can then use this power to choose different words that will propel you to higher levels of success, and you will uncover those hidden beliefs that are holding you back.

"What if there was no demand for others to have the same values as you do? Could you still enjoy decorating the tree?" I asked Sue. "What if you set the tree-decorating night aside for your girlfriends, and you have some holiday cider and some snacks and play some Christmas music while decorating your tree? Make it an annual event. Tell your husband to take the boys shopping or on a 'guys night out.'" Everyone wins. Mom gets a night out with the girls and dad gets a night out with his two sons. Even better, they might go Christmas shopping for mom's gift that night.

Breaking the Agreements

When we get stuck in how it has to be, we eliminate the possibilities of how it might be even better. Every family has collective agreements that no longer serve them.

What is even more interesting are the "collective agreements" we seem to have with other people. These agreements go unnoticed for the most part; take for example the agreement that many people in the Midwest have about winter. On any given day in January or February, you will hear people complaining about winter or the cold weather to come, or talking about past snow storms that made life miserable. "I wish it was spring," or "I will be so happy when winter is over," or "There's nothing to do when the weather is so bad, is so cold," and so on.

One winter, I consciously decided to break that agreement. To do so, I had to respectfully disagree when I heard people complain about the weather. I would say, "I love winter. There are so many things to do in the winter that you either can't do or won't do in the spring or summer. You can work on a book. You can stay inside and read more often. You can make delicious hot soups and have the neighbors over and visit inside by a cozy fire. You can reflect, rest more than usual, clean out your closets and winter clothes. Even though I don't like to be cold, I absolutely love winter clothing!"

When I brought these collective agreements into scrutiny, it seemed to cheer up those who otherwise saw nothing but bad in winter. We have to challenge the collective agreements surrounding us, by asking the question "Do my agreements work for me or against me?" You can only do this if you are conscious of what you agree with, otherwise you will experience outcomes that you do not wish to experience and the reason will be because you agreed with something that does not work for you.

I'll never forget a time when I was able to catch myself and turn a situation around. I had an innovative business concept that I was fleshing out. I turned to a trusted friend and experienced business professional to discuss the concept. Although my friend loved my idea, and has always been a supporter of anything I do, the first thing out of her mouth was negative energy. "The economy is so tight, it might be hard to get enough buyers," she started her conversation. She went on to tell me how others may not understand the project or the concept, and she concluded by talking about how long it would take to materialize the project. On other occasions, I might have walked away disappointed, or I might have tried to convince my friend of the value of my project. This time I just observed. I silently said to myself, "I do not agree. This is one reality and mine is different."

Saying this affirmation to myself kept me conscious so that I didn't fall into a collective agreement (belief) about how things are supposed to be. As a result, the business idea materialized in two days, and there was a profit. In the past I might have focused on the fear and not moved forward simply because I was willing to enter into a "collective agreement" with someone else rather than challenging a belief that did not work for me.

SIGNPOSTS ▶

1. There's no need to justify your beliefs.

2. Beliefs can be challenged and you can change your mind.

3. You are careful about your agreements.

4. You question the "shoulds" and "can'ts" that are keeping you stuck.

5. Life is lived by your own rules and you respect 'other people's rules.

6. It's okay if others disagree with your religion, your weight or hairstyle.

7. You eliminate any belief or behavior that doesn't work for you.

As a child, you have no choice but to obey your parents and to agree to their rules about life, but the agreements you make as a child can block your progress as an adult. As an adult, you have the choice to agree or to disagree, and to create your own rules for life, but you have to be willing to listen.

CHAPTER ELEVEN

Listening

"Listening, not imitation, may be the sincerest form of flattery."

Dr. Joyce Brothers

You can't always see the signs, but you can always hear them. Listening is the best way to know what's really going on with yourself or someone else. Listen closely and you'll hear powerless language full of blame and absent of hope.

Once you develop the power of listening, you can use this power to choose different words and propel yourself forward as you unlock hidden beliefs that are holding you back.

Your language either moves you toward your goals or away from them. One of my favorite consciousness-raising quotes is "Watch your thoughts, for they become words. Watch your words, for they become actions. Watch your actions, for they become habits. Watch your habits, for they become character. Watch your character, for it becomes your destiny."

If you have not yet developed the ability to "listen" to your thoughts, you can go to the next level and simply listen to your words. Notice the symbolic meaning in your life. You may be saying things in jest like, "I just did a stupid thing the other day..." and most of the time your friends will respond by saying something like, "Oh, you are not stupid...why I've done the same thing myself..." Another way we discount ourselves is by saying negative things about our appearance, such as, "I'm gaining so much weight..." What we really hope for is disagreement, and this sort of deprecating talk is really a manipulation tactic to get some needed approval. We secretly expect the person

> Perhaps there is no occasion that we actively seek disagreement so much as when we are discounting ourselves.

whom we are talking with to say, "Oh, you are not gaining weight, don't be ridiculous."

Perhaps there is no occasion that we actively seek disagreement so much as when we are discounting ourselves. If you don't believe me, just try agreeing with someone the next time they are trying to manipulate with self-deprecating talk. "Why, yes, you are stupid, and I see what you mean about gaining all that weight..." I will guarantee that your clever antics will not be liked or appreciated. Listening to your choice of words sheds light on your hidden beliefs. Start asking your friends to help you uncover hidden beliefs and you will be astonished at the treasure of information you will find.

Listening Unlocks Hidden Beliefs

Four of us belong to a mastermind group called ESP, which is an acronym for Entrepreneurial Support Program. The members, Beverly, Marjorie, Patricia and I meet once a month to talk about our businesses and to gain support. Patricia is a great listener. She is present as she listens for more than just the surface meaning. One particular day when the four of us were meeting, I shared a business deal I wanted to propose, and then I asked the group for feedback. Patricia said, "The idea is great, but I think you need to listen to the words that you used. You said, 'I'm going to weasel my way in with this company.'" Patricia continued, "You don't need to weasel, and I've never known you to weasel your way in, because that does not represent integrity or authentic power. What you have to offer is good and worthy."

My first reaction was total surprise, then defense. "Well, I didn't really mean that I was trying to do anything underhanded. I just meant that I want to construct a strategy instead of shooting from the hip." As you might be thinking, there is a vast difference between constructing a strategy and weaseling your way in the door! Of course, Patricia knows me and acknowledged that the ornery part of me likes to use words like "weasel" to get a laugh or to provoke discussion. Patricia knows that there is a part of me that likes to instigate a bit of drama through the use of

> "Does this behavior, thought, or activity move me toward a loving relationship or away from it?"

exaggeration, but that's not the point. Perhaps there is a hidden belief about business deals being shady, or perhaps there was a tiny fragment of a belief that to be successful means that you have to be sneaky and under the radar, instead of upfront and forthright.

Words are important and deserve our attention. Count yourself lucky if you have friends who listen to you and hold you accountable for the words you use.

Listening to your thoughts opens the door to many opportunities. Listening to others increases your intuitive abilities and allows you to give one of the most precious gifts to another.

If listening is such a good tool for building relationships, why don't people do a better job of it? Listening to others can be time consuming. Listening to others can be boring. Listening to others can be painful. If we would just admit it, most of us are self-absorbed and we prefer a different topic of conversation—ourselves. Like Toby Keith, the country singer says in his hit song, "I want to talk about me, I want to talk about I, I want to talk about number one, oh my, me, mine, what I think, what I like, what I know, what I want, what I see." Of course we pretend that we are interested, as the song so poignantly points out, "I like talking about you, you, you, you, usually, but occasionally I want to talk about me."

In reality, most of us like talking about ourselves most of the time and occasionally we stop to hear what the other person has to say. Point is, when the topic isn't about us, instead of paying attention, we interject our opinions, dispense advice or twist the topic back to yours truly. Listening requires self-discipline.

Listening to others influences your life as a parent, a spouse, a boss or a friend. Listen between the lines for the emotion and the hidden meanings behind the words. A fun exercise is to listen to the way others talk about time. You hear variations of "I would, but I don't have the time," which is a sign of not taking full responsibility for the choices available. In other words, this is victim language. You also hear people give away their power to other people, for example, "He made me mad," which indicates that others are responsible for your emotional responses and so on.

Louise Hay has a wonderful book entitled *You Can Heal Your Life*, and in the book is a chapter that explains the connection between the physical and emotional. If you listen closely, you intuitively know what's going on with your friends, coworkers and family. Many times you can directly see a mind-body connection between the words that are spoken.

The Mind-Body Connection

When you listen to friends or family, listen for statements such as "He is a pain in the neck," or "I'm sick and tired." Notice how often the person who uses the words "sick and tired" is actually physically sick and or tired. You might be amazed at the power of words and how connected we are to creating our own realities.

Belinda, a friend and business associate, was having a difficult time at work. In addition, she was struggling with some relationship issues with her significant other. Belinda, when recounting the information to me would say, "I just couldn't stand it any longer." Then Belinda told me that during this time, she had to have surgery on her foot and was laid up in bed for three months. I couldn't help but see the metaphysical correlation. I can't "stand" it, correlated with no longer being able to physically stand on her own two feet. These conversations are spoken but not often listened to. No doubt Belinda had many silent conversations about how she couldn't stand her situation, and how that played out in her physical condition, but it never occurred to her until we discussed it. Your level of listening will affect the quality and depth of your relationships, and a side benefit is that good listening is healing.

> If you listen closely, you intuitively know what's going on with your friends, coworkers and family.

Listening is an Act of Love

I witnessed the power of listening one time at a social event that my mom attended with me. Mom and I met a woman named Mary who was going through some personal distress, including making medical decisions for her aging mother who was in the hospital with no hope of recovering, and with health issues too severe to consider home care.

Mary's frail body shook with anxiety as she shared her sorrow and frustrations of accepting the doctor's recommendation to put her mother in a nursing home. Mary talked about how she longed to please her mother, who still had all her mental faculties, how difficult it was to make this decision as she reversed roles with her mother, the daunting task of finding the best nursing home and the overwhelming task of dealing with financial issues. In the midst of Mary's story, another person joined in giving her two cents' worth with suggestions beginning with phrases such as, "What you really need to do," and "If I were you..."

In contrast, I observed my mother listening without interrupting, nodding occasionally without offering any advice. She gave complete attention to the woman who was speaking. She avoided the temptation to say, "I know how you feel," or "I've been there too," or "I just lost my own mother two months ago."

It would have been easy for my mom to have shifted the conversation with tales of her own grief since she had just buried her own mother, my grandmother, only a few months earlier, and had dealt with some of the same issues that Mary was facing. Instead she stayed in the present moment, giving her full attention to Mary.

Although I was observing and absorbing Mary's information, I also struggled against the urge to "rescue" or help Mary fix the situation. It was all I could do not to offer advice such as where she could find the best nursing home and what she should expect as things progressed. Even though I was conscious of my internal struggle to be in the moment and just listen, a little bit of "unconsciousness" leaked out as I said, "Well you are talking to someone who has just been through what you are going through," referring to my mother. "You two need to exchange phone numbers," I said again, adding my two cents.

My mom finally spoke. "Mary, the best thing you can do is to do your research and look at as many nursing homes as you possibly can. Ask questions so that you can be sure in your own mind that you made the right decision for you, because everyone's situation is different." Intuitively, my mother knew that Mary didn't need sympathy. Mary didn't need to be fixed. Mary needed the healing power of listening.

The biggest gift you can give to someone else is to be present and truly listen, and the biggest way to propel your own success is to listen to yourself. Listening is an act of love.

SIGNPOSTS ▶

1. You recognize the power of words.

2. You monitor your self-talk and speak kindly about yourself and others.

3. Being the center of attention is no longer a requirement.

4. You no longer need to have all the answers.

5. Everyone else seems to be a horrible listener.

6. It exhausts you when you are around a chatty Cathy.

7. You recognize that you used to drain other people by talking too much.

8. People are energized, and feel understood when they are around you.

The greatest gift you can give to yourself or others is your attention. You give this gift by listening. Listening to your inner dialogue is important because you can observe how the voice in your head influences your behaviors. You can witness the creative force of language by hearing how you declare yourself to the world by the simple words "I am."

When you have the discipline to listen to others without judgment, advice or interruption, they feel understood, energized and most of all, loved.

Chapter Twelve

Choices

"The strongest principle of growth lies in human choice."

George Eliot

Re-inventing your life requires you to make conscious choices instead of blindly accepting other people's beliefs, following the rules or living for others. As exciting as it is to re-invent your life, re-invention takes commitment. You have to be willing to do what is required, whether that means learning new skills, expanding your comfort zone, or changing your beliefs. Whether you are re-inventing your image, your family life, your financial status, your physical appearance or your romantic life, make no mistake, every commitment is eventually tested. A sign that you have been tested and failed is the regret you feel after having done something that takes you further away from the outcome you want.

No one has ever said, "I wish I'd have charged more on my credit card."

No one ever said, "I wish I'd have had one more drink, had one more helping of dessert, slept with him sooner, screamed at her louder, or let him take advantage of me one more time." Yet every day someone overextends their credit, drinks too much, has one more helping of dessert, has a one-night stand, or continues to abuse or to be abused one more time.

Every day people make commitments as an effort to re-invent some part of their lives, but **just as many commitments are broken as there are commitments made.** Broken commitments often lead to regrets later. Why do people make a commitment only to break it later?

Commitments versus Feelings

A commitment is more than a wish or a feeling. The way you feel one moment can change in the next. Talk and ideas are easy, but action is often difficult. Commitments and decisions define who you are and are based on the big picture. The reason people don't keep commitments is because they don't consider the consequences of their actions and they act only on their immediate feelings. The emotional journey is not about being a slave to your emotions. The emotional journey is about learning to interpret what your emotions are teaching you.

People cancel plans just because they don't feel like following through. People have an affair just because they feel lonely or because they feel attracted. Decisions made from a feeling in-the-moment are not likely to yield positive results. People have regrets because their choices were made based on winning little instead of winning big.

Unconscious choices are based on the need to prove a point, win an argument or the need to be right about a particular situation. In other words, there is often a hidden agenda that masks the stated commitment.

Finding Truth

There is a saying that there are different levels of truth at different levels of consciousness. What this means is that you can find a kernel of truth from any particular point of view. We waste a lot of energy trying to find the kernel of truth so that we can successfully protect our view of the world.

If you question this statement, then I challenge you to think back to a time you had an argument with someone. The most natural thing to do is to tell your side of the story to your friends so that you can get agreement about being right. Being right is a way to justify bad behavior instead of rising to excellence and making choices based on the highest way to represent yourself.

Some acquaintances of mine, Karla and Craig, were having some tumultuous times in their marriage. Karla confided to her closest group of friends that she had decided to have an affair with Mike, a coworker whom she had developed a deep friendship with in dealing with her personal problems. Karla justified the decision by saying that her husband had done the same thing to her two years prior. Karla forgot her original commitment and was making her decision based on what her husband did two years ago!

> If you want to become excellent, you have to quit worrying about being right.

Karla's new commitment was getting revenge or perhaps her real commitment was making excuses for wrong behavior. There's no doubt that Karla has friends who listen to her and see her reasoning, or at the least understand her urge for revenge, however there is no real solution in Karla having an affair just to get even.

On the contrary, Karla would most likely regret the decision and would dislike the consequences sure to follow.

Being Right versus Being Excellent

When your goal is to be "right", you forfeit the opportunity to be excellent. The need to win, or the need to be right keeps many relationships from the success that could otherwise follow. You know you are on the wrong side of the tracks when you want to justify your decisions or get agreement about your position as a former client, Rick, did when he approached me to discuss his situation.

> By your choices, you reveal your commitments.

Re-invention is sometimes the only choice to salvage a relationship. Rick and Sherry's marriage was in need of a re-invention or the outcome would be divorce. The main problem was Rick's attitude about his wife's relationship with her son Jake.

Rick married Sherry when Jake was 16, but Jake decided to live with his grandmother so that he could complete high school in his district. As a result, Jake and Rick never really bonded, and Sherry often overcompensated at times by giving Jake gifts or money without discussing it with Rick. Sherry and Rick continually disagree on issues involving Jake. As a result, Jake avoids Rick. The drama has continued over the last six years, but has not had that big of an impact because Jake has been away at college.

At 22, Jake is graduating college and Rick has declared that he will not attend the graduation of a "spoiled mama's boy" who hasn't had the courtesy to come to visit for two years. Rick has started acting like a judge and jury while entering into a power struggle with his wife. Upon hearing Rick's decision, Sherry walked out on their marriage and moved in with her mother. Rick consulted with me wanting to know who was right and who was wrong.

The first thing I said to Rick was, "If you want to be excellent, quit worrying about being right. Asking who is right and who is wrong is the wrong question to be asking. The right question to ask is, 'What are you committed to?'"

I continued on, "If you are committed to being right then that commitment requires the behaviors and beliefs that are creating the current situation. However, if you are committed to supporting Sherry in the love she has for her only son, or if you are committed to kindness, or showing love, then that commitment requires an entirely different set of actions and beliefs, and would require you to adjust your attitude and your beliefs so that you can re-invent your family life."

Actions speak louder than words. The little choices you make moment by moment reveal to you what your intentions and motives are, regardless of what you say they are. As I mentioned before, each person has a philosophy about winning whether they articulate that philosophy or not. The signs can be witnessed in the conscious and unconscious choices that play out.

The facts are clear in Rick's case. Rick was focused on winning little instead of winning big. Rick's commitment is to winning an argument instead of a commitment to honoring the relationships in his life.

Rick was more concerned with his own ego than he was with his wife or with his future relationship with his stepson. However, Rick was inconsiderate of his commitments and Rick cannot be responsible until he recognizes his choices. The right question is intended to bring about consciousness and offer Rick some new choices. None of us can be truly responsible until we live by our values and commitments.

If you are not sure what you are committed to, all you need to do is to look at your choices. Your choices reveal your commitments. One of the biggest and most important commitments I have ever made is the commitment to relationships. All of life is based on relationships. Show me any topic and I can show you a direct or indirect link to relationships. For example, being a parent is about building a trusting relationship with your children. Belonging to a church is about building a community of support to worship together.

The most important question you can ask yourself in regard to your important relationships is, "Does this behavior, thought, or activity move me toward a loving relationship or away from it?"

That is all you need ask. From those answers, your course of action to re-invention will take care of itself. A mutually-beneficial relationship with your friends, coworkers and boss will be filled with integrity, laughter, fun, and honesty. Will you have problems, disagreements and

> The facts speak for themselves, regardless of the reasons.

challenges? Absolutely, but the problems, challenges and disagreements won't be the theme of your relationship. The same principles apply to relationships at home.

A loving relationship with your children is a benefit to them and to you. It benefits you to look after and serve the best interests of your spouse. At the same time, it benefits your spouse to treat you lovingly and look out for your best interests. Dr. Phil McGraw says the best way to get a good wife is to be a good husband, and the best way to get a great husband is to be the best wife.

Mutually-rewarding relationships benefit two people, you and the person with whom you share your life. A mutually-rewarding relationship is an equation of equality that can be determined by asking these questions:

1. Does this elationship offer equal benefits for both people involved?

2. Are both of us free from verbal and physical abuse?

3. Do we each show respect and hold each other in high regard?

4. Are we equally committed in thought, word and action?

5. Does this relationship bring out my best qualities?

6. Does this relationship support my growth and development?

A "yes" answer to all of these questions eliminates the possibility of living with an abusive partner as a victim or enabling someone to take advantage of you through deceit, destructive patterns or unhealthy habits.

Answering these questions helps you assess where you are and what changes you might need to make. Re-inventing your relationships requires you to answer tough questions and make solid commitments. You are as successful as the commitments you make. Remember when I said that everyone has a philosophy about winning? You can't hide your life philosophy or your commitments because by your choices, you REVEAL your commitments. Every thing you say is a representation of you.

Your Choices Reveal Your Commitments

When someone tells you that you have a bad attitude and you say, "I couldn't help it, I've had a bad day," you represent yourself as one who makes excuses instead of one who solves problems. When you raise your voice at your spouse or your employee, you represent yourself as one who has no discipline over your emotions. When you argue with someone without seeing another point of view, you represent yourself as one who has a strong need to be right. When you monopolize a conversation, you represent yourself as one who does not know how to listen. This is true whether you are aware of your incessant talking or whether you are unaware of it. When you gloat over one of your successes, you represent yourself as one who is insensitive to the feelings of others. When you show up 30 minutes late, you represent yourself as one who doesn't respect the time of others.

When you fail to follow through, when you make a promise you can't keep, or when you say something you regret, just remember that you are representing yourself. You represent yourself as one who is not aware, as one who can not follow through, as one who has no focus, as one who can not be taken seriously, and so on. You get the picture.

The Facts

Perhaps as you are reading this you are making arguments. You are saying, "There are reasons why I am late," or "I was right when I raised my voice," or "I wouldn't have gloated if it hadn't been done to me in the first place." While you are focusing on excuses and emotions, I am not judging your reasons; I am simply stating the facts and showing you a mirror of how you are revealing yourself to the world.

You were either on time or late. You either listened or you didn't. You either held your temper or blew your stack. You either won with grace or you didn't. The facts speak for themselves regardless of the reasons. Success is a given. You will be as successful as that to which you are committed. The question is, what are you committed to?

SIGNPOSTS ▶

1. Your choices no longer lead to regret.

2. Other points of view become interesting.

3. Apologizing is a skill that comes in handy.

4. Thinking first eliminates the need to apologize later.

5. You quit making excuses and require more of yourself.

6. You start to feel good about your choices.

7. You are able to disagree and still maintain the relationship.

8. Relationships are a priority, but not at the expense of yourself.

9. Others in your life start stepping up their game as well.

You represent yourself to your fullest potential when what you think, say and do are in complete alignment. This happens when you live your commitments.

If you are not completely sure what you are committed to, then all you have to do is look at your choices because by your choices, you reveal your commitment. Every temptation to make a bad choice and every negative reaction that comes to the surface is your teacher to help you on the path, if you can but recognize your teachers.

CHAPTER THIRTEEN

Teachers

"When the student is ready, the teacher will appear."
Buddhist Proverb

Desire or desperation is always the driver of re-invention. In other words, you are always re-inventing either out of conscious choice or because circumstances demand that you change.

Change is a combination of four elements: expected, unexpected, wanted and unwanted. Buying a new house, marrying the person of your dreams, having a baby, or leaving an unsatisfactory relationship are all examples of change that we might classify as "good" change. Sometimes "good" change is planned and sometimes "good" change is unexpected.

Change can be also unwanted and unexpected such as getting a divorce, aging, losing a loved one, or getting transferred to another location in your job. When "bad" changes happen, you re-invent your life out of necessity.

Choices

Regardless of the kinds of changes currently happening in your life, and whether you planned for the changes or not, you have choices in your response to change. You can accept it, plan for it, resist it, deny it, go with the flow, or you can evolve with and create new changes. When circumstances change and you resist the flow, it is as if the music has changed but you continue dancing to the old rhythm.

> "When the music changes, so does the dance."
> ~ African Proverb

Nonetheless, life always presents you with opportunities to grow and expand. These opportunities show up as teachers, wise masters who help you to learn the next thing you need to learn on your journey from Point A to Point B.

Here's the tricky part: You will not always identify your teachers right away. Sometimes the teacher is a person and other times the teacher is a situation. For example, if you need to learn the lesson of patience, you will be supplied just the right teacher in the form of a situation suited to help you learn.

You will be in a hurry, but there will be a slowpoke who sits through a green light while you fume. Or as you hungrily wait in line at a restaurant, you become frustrated that the server doesn't even know you exist.

A sign that you are have not learned the next lesson is when you feel stuck and the lesson keeps repeating itself. For example, you respond with road rage at the slowpoke in traffic, or you throw a fit with the oblivious server. You're not really stuck; you're just resisting learning from your teachers. Another way to say it is when you go through significant changes, your "stuff" surfaces. This is especially true when you make conscious choices to re-invent or heal old patterns. Make no mistake, your new commitments are going to be tested.

Take my friend Shauna, for example. When Shauna became pregnant with her first child, she made a commitment to become a nurturing mother and to be full of love and laughter. What Shauna did not realize was in order to fulfill the commitment to be a loving, nurturing mother, she must first learn the lessons of forgiveness. Once Shauna gave birth to her daughter, old childhood resentments and anger surfaced. Shauna recalled numerous mistakes her own mother had made.

Why did Shauna's resentments surface? Shauna had made a commitment right before the birth of her daughter to forgive her own mother for some past hurts and misunderstandings. Because Shauna made a commitment to forgive, she became challenged to keep that commitment. Shauna, an insightful woman, realized that you can't be loving when you are carrying around old baggage.

Claiming Your Power

When you make a commitment, your choices will have to stretch you so that you can continue to gain power from those choices. Your commitment doesn't need to be as dramatic or as personal as Shauna's. Say, for example, you get the vision and commitment to get promoted in your company. That would be an expected and wanted change that you are seeking. You know your work is excellent and your attendance record is above reproach. You see yourself enjoying the additional income and you also want the respect and prestige that comes with the position.

> Here's the tricky part: You will not always identify your teachers right away.

You interview and you don't get the job. Now you are disappointed, but because you have consciously committed to moving forward, you look for the lesson and you ask the boss what you could have done better. You then find out that the only reason you didn't get the position is because of a small character flaw you had never addressed. Your boss felt that although perfect as you are, you are way too impatient and he says, "Your work is great, but we expect our leaders to have more self-control and patience." So you make a commitment to become more patient and you say a silent prayer, "God, make me more patient."

The Teacher Appears

The next day you are driving to an important appointment. You know that you don't do well when you are on an empty stomach, and you also know that you are committed to eating healthy food. Your dilemma is to grab something healthy and quick, so you spot the fast food restaurant and think about a salad, but you notice the line is wrapped around the block and know that you can't wait that long. You find a healthy eatery just around the corner, so you hop out hoping to be in and out in 10 minutes. When you get inside, you see that the person being served can't make up her mind and the person in front of you is ordering for their corporate office. In the past you would have rolled your eyes and looked at your watch. Or you might have asked everyone in line if you could go ahead and go first, just this once. You might have even stormed out in anger. What do you do?

Do you even recognize that you have choices, or do you revert back to old patterns? Do you call your appointment and say you are running 10 minutes late, or do you risk giving your presentation on an empty stomach, which usually only feeds on your own impatience?

It doesn't matter so much about the food, or the obstacles in place. What matters is that you notice the sign. The sign is that the Universe is supplying you with the lesson of patience. You didn't think that because of one intention and one quick prayer that you are magically going to change your personality overnight, did you?

Passing the Test

If you are quick to recognize this lesson, you will have an "ah-ha" moment, and that alone will make the frustration worth it all. You can then say a quick prayer of "thanks" as you make new decisions and new commitments. You have passed the test and this means you won't have to keep repeating the same lesson! This is the way you can speed up your growth by noticing the lesson and by passing the tests that life gives you.

Unfortunately, we usually miss the lesson dozens of time before we see the patterns. We blame the restaurant, or we justify why we were in a hurry instead of realizing that we are getting what we are asking for. We set an intention to become more patient and the Universe says, "Well, here is a class designed specifically for you and it's called Patience 101, and it will require that you show up as patient in the most stressful of circumstances."

Of course you will always also be supplied with a few friends who will scoff at your dilemma and tell you how working on an empty stomach would never stress them out at all. These comments deflate your balloon and make you feel that you will never get it right. You may also be blessed with friends who totally agree with your point of view.

Your Lesson Plan is Tailored

What you need to keep in mind is that this lesson plan was developed only for you, not for anyone else. Each person's lessons are tailored to his or her needs, so there is no point getting into a conversation about who is more patient or what someone else would or would not do. All lessons are meant to help you get from where you are to where you are supposed to go.

However, most of us have lots of illusions about getting from Point A to Point B and the whole concept of the universe supplying the necessary teachers and lessons. At times, you mistake the teacher and view your teachers as obstacles that are holding you back. This was certainly true for me in the factory. I was committed to re-inventing my life. I knew I wanted to be a trainer and my business name would be ICARE, which stood for, "Improving Communication and Relationships Everywhere."

I couldn't wait to get out of the factory where I could really practice the art of good communication and relationship building. I had noticed how often in my "factory life" there was so much conflict and misunderstanding. My vision at the time was that somehow I could teach supervisors how to inspire others instead of intimidating them.

I remember saying, "You can't improve communication and relationships in a factory when you have a boss that yells and screams at you." This boss didn't excel at the art of problem solving or teamwork. In fact, when employees would approach him with a problem he had three standard answers: "There's nothing I can do. That's just the way it is." and, "If you don't like it, find another place to work." Out of frustration, I would also say, "You can't reason with a rock," and that became my excuse not to try to become a better communicator. I felt at the time that this "rock" was my obstacle. In reality, all the people in my life at that time were there to help me keep my new commitments.

Doing What is Required

What many people fail to realize is this: Each commitment brings with it certain requirements. For example, my new commitment to improve communication and relationships everywhere required of me the willingness to approach a supervisor who seemed difficult to work with. A commitment to eating more healthy meals requires you to bring your lunch to work or to eat differently than your family. It is important to know the requirements of any commitment.

For example, a commitment to staying married is different than a commitment to having a great marriage. The requirements for "staying" married might mean ignoring real problems, putting up with abuse or sacrificing yourself to please another. The commitment to a "happy marriage" requires that you sometimes face difficult situations, have difficult conversations and sometimes that requirement makes you examine your commitment to the relationship.

Many times we avoid keeping commitments by believing that we will be more able to keep the commitment once certain conditions line out. In my case, I believed that communication in the "real world" would be different than communication in my "factory world." The challenge is to re-invent from the inside instead of demanding circumstances change first.

SIGNPOSTS▶

1. You become more aware of the rhythms of your life.

2. There is a new awareness of your own resistance or flow to changes.

3. Manifesting what you want becomes easier.

4. Sometimes you repeat a lesson.

5. You understand each commitment has requirements attached.

6. Teachers are not always kind, but they always add value.

7. Life is fun and ntertaining when you identify your teachers.

At some point on your journey, you will make significant changes, either by choice or circumstances. Re-invention always involves change, which you can accept or resist. Throughout your journey, you will have many teachers to help you get from Point A to Point B. Your teachers wear many disguises, but it is up to you to identify your teachers quickly so that you don't have to repeat the more difficult lessons.

CHAPTER FOURTEEN

Forgiveness

"Suffering is always the effect of wrong thought in some direction. It is an indication that the individual is out of harmony with himself, with the Law of his being."

James Allen

Re-invention, whether done out of conscious choice or out of necessity, is difficult. When you are learning something new, you feel vulnerable and worry about how others will judge you. The spiral down begins when you start judging yourself, which is the wrong thought, and that brings about suffering both in your inner and outer world.

Big changes challenge you to your core as self-doubt and old tapes start playing in your head reminding you of past failures. According to hundreds of surveys, it appears that over 70% of us admit to being hard on ourselves. We constantly beat ourselves up for the way we look, our level of competence, our background, our lack of experience, and even what we just said 15 minutes ago. The harder we are on ourselves, the more judgmental we are toward others as well. The outcome is that life becomes more restricted. Have you ever wondered what to do when you feel stuck? Feeling stuck, blocked or restricted is a sign that you need to practice some forgiveness.

Judgment Blocks Prosperity

Judgment blocks prosperity, and forgiveness opens the flow. Even an assumption can swiftly turn into judgment. For example, you assume a certain level of customer service at a restaurant and when you don't get it, you let that experience become the basis of how you feel for the rest of the day. Instead of accepting or fixing the situation, you go around complaining and pouting about

> Judgment blocks prosperity, and forgiveness opens the flow.

your poor service and your mood spirals downward on the emotional scale, only to leave you feeling worse than had you not had the disappointment that comes from an unmet expectation.

I have experienced the stagnation of judgment and the ultimate release once forgiveness was rendered. My first real experience with this concept happened early in my speaking career when I started getting engagements that required me travel to places like Washington, D.C., and New York. Being from the Midwest, I had never taken a subway or a cab. I wasn't sure about the etiquette for tipping bellmen, and so on. Although these are simply facts, I judged myself as being unsophisticated. Had I known what I know now, I could have just lightened up and enjoyed the opportunity to learn and experience. Nonetheless, my first experience in Washington, D.C. to speak at a NASA event totally changed my perceptions about forgiveness and why we should give ourselves unconditional acceptance so that we can be in the flow.

My plane landed at the Ronald Regan National airport, and I got a blue shuttle with six other people and headed to my hotel. Each person was going to a different hotel and the driver, who barely spoke English, started mapping out his direction. "I'm at Capitol on the Hill," I said, knowing that it was a Holiday Inn.

When I was dropped off at the hotel, I asked one last time for reassurance, "Is this the Capital on the Hill?" To which the driver nodded affirmatively as he handed me my bag. I felt scattered as I fumbled around looking for my wallet to give a tip. Before I had a chance to collect my thoughts and thank the shuttle driver, he jumped back in his van and sped away.

Distracted by the big city, the tip paying and the bellman who was trailing off with my bag, I looked away for a split second while the driver took off with my bag that had my clothes in it. To top it off, I didn't get a receipt.

In a panic, I rushed to explain my dilemma to the front-desk concierge. I remembered one of the passengers saying they were going to the Hyatt, so I asked the concierge to call the Hyatt so that I could get the shuttle driver to bring back my bags. When the concierge handed me the phone to speak to the Hyatt front desk, my frustration mounted and my thoughts were racing as I tried to explain my situation to the Hyatt concierge.

"My name is Marlene Chism, and the Blue Shuttle that is coming to your hotel has my bag. He just dropped me off at the Holiday on the Hill, and I would like to see if he could bring my bag back immediately."

The front-desk concierge corrected me, "You are not at the Holiday on the Hill. You are at the Holiday Capitol."

I shrieked to the concierge on the other line, "I'm not even at the right hotel! I'm at Holiday Capitol." My assumption was that the shuttle driver would know how to get me to the correct hotel! That is a reasonable assumption and the initial disappointment is expected, but at some point, even when disappointed, you only have two choices: Accept it or fix it.

"Can you have him return my bags to the Holiday Capitol?" I asked the Hyatt concierge.

"Consider it done," he said on the other end of the phone line.

Although I had the Hyatt concierge's word, I did not consider it done. My past experience with travel was a reminder that promises made and promises delivered depend not so much on the integrity of the person making the promise, but upon the culture of the person making the promise. You cannot assume that people from other cultures hold the same values as you. In some cultures, it is considered bad manners not to give you the answer you want to hear, so as a result, you are likely to hear wrong directions or empty promises just to make you happy in the moment.

Anxiety crept in and I could feel my immune system weakening. I sat down to process the information. It dawned on me that I might not see my bags until the next day, which would be too late. What would I wear to the workshop? How could I use the rest of the day to prepare for this mishap? All kinds of stories started invading my peace as my mind left the present moment and wandered aimlessly into the future.

Resistance Blocks the Flow

Then consciousness came back to me and I realized I was not thinking correctly about the situation. What would I teach if this was a seminar and the lost bag and wrong hotel dilemma was someone else's problem? What would I tell someone else to do if his or her life was not in the flow? I would say, "Take responsibility for all the circumstances in your life, and trust that you can manifest what you want."

> In order to become responsible, you first have to recognize your choices.

In order to become responsible, you first have to recognize your choices. Responsibility is the recognition of choice. Otherwise you simply react from all of your wrongful thinking. I would ask, "What are your choices?"

I could take a cab to the right hotel so that I could get settled in. The problem with that was that now the bag was coming back to the wrong hotel and I'd probably have to pay another cab fee to get the bag there. That would mean three cab fees simply because of the mistake of the shuttle driver. I didn't like that solution.

The next choice is to wait. I may have to wait three hours. Depression started to settle in, and I felt my eyes get wet. I realized I was stuck and my life was not flowing. I was resisting the present moment.

Gary Zukav, author of *The Heart of the Soul*, says that **stress is the consequence of resistance to your life**. I was definitely resisting. When you resist, that means you need to own your stuff. It means you have forgiveness work to do so that you can allow the flow of life to come to you.

I decided to forgive the shuttle driver. "He barely speaks English, and didn't mean to run off with my bags," I reasoned.

That forgiveness didn't do much for me. I didn't really feel much resentment to begin with. There is nothing to forgive if you didn't condemn in the first place.

What could it be? Where am I holding a negative judgment? At that moment, it dawned on me and I said, "I forgive myself for not being a sophisticated traveler."

Immediately the shuttle driver circled around to pick me up and take me to the right hotel. This is how the magic of forgiveness opens the life flow.

Opening the Flow

The other example that comes to mind is when I was in New York with my friend Julie. I had previously met another woman named Jennifer, a savvy business-woman who had agreed to take Julie and me on a tour of the city while we were visiting.

Julie and I were dying to see the Broadway play "Wicked." We found out that tickets were $100, but we were still willing to pay. Once we arrived at the ticket counter, we were told that tickets were sold out for three months.

However, the ticket person said that every day they have a lottery if we didn't mind waiting around for 30 minutes. Jennifer said she had another hour before she had to go into the Bronx, and she would wait with us and even enter the lottery herself. This gave us three chances to win one of the 25 sets of tickets.

While we waited, we conversed more with Jennifer and learned about her business. Julie and I enjoyed hearing about Jennifer's business, and I especially enjoyed it because she was letting me in on all of the relationship drama that was currently going on. I could easily spot the areas that were blocking Jennifer's flow, and eventually the opportunity opened for me to teach her some of the concepts that I teach in my management consulting practice. I also shared with Jennifer the concepts of how judgment blocks prosperity and how to identify the power struggles, and so on. Jennifer, being a highly-educated woman, caught on very quickly and the conversation was lively and stimulating.

Finally the announcer told the crowd the drawing was about to commence. The three of us stood up and listened to name after name being called. It appeared that we weren't going to be winners after all.

I let out a sigh and said, "Oh well, it was worth a try." At that very moment Jennifer said, "Hey, don't judge and block the flow."

All three of us simultaneously took a deep breath and immediately Jennifer's name was called out as the winner of the tickets. Time and time again, I have experienced letting go of judgment and then immediately following, some sort of magic happens.

SIGNPOSTS ▶

1. Doubt creeps in and distorts your perspective.

2. Stress occurs in the form of resistance.

3. Negative thoughts about self or others preoccupy your mind.

4. Release comes through acceptance or forgiveness.

5. Life starts flowing when judgment ceases.

Acceptance is a part of forgiveness. When you hold grudges against yourself or someone else, your energy gets blocked. This blockage shows up in the circumstances of your life and the feeling of anxiety, which often leads to physical problems, or even illness.

If you feel stuck, the easiest way to break the spell is to figure out what you are judging and make peace with the other person, the circumstances or that part of yourself that needs to be healed.

Letting go of judgment may not enable you to win lottery tickets, or get your lost bags back with no hassles. Perhaps these were coincidences that happened to me when I was learning these lessons. Never think that your lessons are about the circumstances, manipulating others or changing your luck. The real magic in letting go of judgment is in how you are more able to cope with and take charge of your life. When your life is flowing, you experience the every day miracles of life instead of being stuck in negativity.

EPILOGUE

Happiness

"If your success is not on your own terms, if it looks good to the world but does not feel good in your heart, it is not success at all."
Anna Quindlen

Life always offers signs and lessons. It is up to you to interpret the message. A day will come when you realize you have accomplished many of the things that you set out to do, yet you continue to want more and more. That is the nature of expansion and growth, and the very reason you will always be in a state of re-invention.

The problem arises when you wrongly believe that the next achievement will make you happy. This illusion keeps you striving for the next level, which promises to be your salvation.

Much of the time our unhappiness is due to compulsive thinking about success, judging our current level of success, and the obsession to achieve the next big success.

Happiness can be experienced immediately once the success question is taken off the table. This realization came to me one day in my daily ritual of prayer and journaling.

I was obsessing about the success question and I did something very dangerous: I started comparing myself to others. My journaling revealed judgments

> Happiness is never a result of success. Success is the result of happiness.

about why I didn't have a book and why others were making more money than me and why I didn't take the traditional path of education and so on. My thinking was focused on what I didn't have and what I hadn't done instead of being grateful for all of my successes and growth." By the way, journaling is one of the self-awareness tools I teach in my training programs to help people reclaim their power and focus. You must get control of negative energy, wrong thinking, and drama patterns such as complaining and comparing yourself to othersHave you ever noticed how comparing yourself to others never results in a winning situation?

The judgments you place on yourself or others only offers two outcomes: You will feel miserable or superior. From that state of consciousness, you cannot be of service to others. When you find yourself lapsing into "comparison mode" it's time to stop the drama and take a step back. Quit pretending that you can judge your life or your situation by anyone else's life or situation.

Take a trip down memory lane and pat yourself on the back for all that YOU have accomplished. You will most likely find that what you are doing right now would have been considered the epitome of success five or 10 years ago.

Just a few years ago, I was working in a factory, doing everything from packing cheese on the lines, to tearing down equipment for sanitation, to driving a forklift, to stacking skids. During those years, I would have said that if I could only find a career that I loved, if I could only get out of my blue-collar job, if I only had more choices, more fun, more opportunities, a better education, chances to travel and experience the rest of the world then I would be successful and that success would make me feel happy. Then it dawned on me that I had already done those things and it still wasn't enough.

I had finished my college degree and a master's degree. I had traveled across the United States from Seattle, Washington, to Long Island, New York. Several times I had spoken at such places as NASA headquarters in Washington, D.C., and NASA's Goddard Space Flight Center. I had developed friends in almost every state I have visited, and I had developed products that have been purchased by Fortune 500 companies such as The Detroit Free Press and DTE Energy. I had already been interviewed by radio stations and had articles published in trade magazines. Not bad for a former factory worker who spent 21 years packing cheese, taking 15-minute breaks and looking up a the clock to see if it was time to rotate!

In just a few short years, I went from no freedom to virtually no boundaries. It was possible to sleep late, skip work, and make any decision that I see fit. Yet, no matter how much I had accomplished, it seemed that the "real" success that would result in my being happy was always right around the corner.

Identity Crisis

I asked myself, "Who would I be without my career?" It occurred to me that I had left one identity, that of being a factory worker, for another identity, that of being a professional speaker and writer. Neither identity was the source of my happiness.

I decided to take the summer off. No more work. I wanted to see what it would feel like to not base my happiness on the amount of business I booked or how busy I was able to be. During this sabbatical, I had some big insights. At first it was like I was grieving. My old self was dying, and now happiness had to come from just being me. I had to find joy in just being around people, in having nothing to do, nowhere to go.

That is when I realized that I had it backwards all along. Happiness is never a result of success. **Success is the result of happiness.** Once you realize that you are already successful, going to the next level is just a game. You can observe the signs that you are growing, and when you are in the valley, you start to get excited because you know you are getting ready for the next level.

Or, if you are on the mountain and in your comfort zone, you can consciously choose to stay on the mountain longer or to move to the next level.

As a culture and individually, we get wound up in false identities we create for ourselves. We become our titles, our careers, our income or our education. We are constantly seeking the standing ovation, the approval from others. The problem is that no matter what you achieve, there is always someone better, richer, more educated or more talented or more blessed, and often, even when you do your very best, sometimes you don't get the promotion, the standing ovation or the title. So why not commit to happiness first so that you can start to enjoy the success you already have and open the flow to receiving more?

Your Power is in the Present

So often we spend time daydreaming about the past or wishing for the future, yet as Louise Hay says, "The point of power is always in the present moment." We forget this point, and instead we imagine the future as our savior and we wait for success to make us happy, instead of living in the present moment and enjoying each step.

"When I get the promotion, then I'll be happy. When I lose the weight, then I'll be happy. When I have some free time, then I'll be happy. When I get another job, then I'll be happy. When I get rid of the problem employee, then I'll be happy. If my kid ever graduates, then I'll be happy. If I get the standing

*ovation then I'll be happy. If I figure out what I want
in life, then I'll be happy."*

There seems to be an agreement that success comes
in future, and once that future arrives, happiness is sure
to follow. In a nutshell, we believe that happiness is the
result of some kind of success or event. The weight loss,
the promotion, the free time or new job represents the
success that will lead to happiness. More often than not,
we place our "happiness" in the hands of fate, or in the
hands of things we have no control over.

Sometimes we even depend upon the approval of
others to make ourselves feel successful. If we do get the
approval, we feel successful and that success translates
into happiness. If we fail to get the approval of others,
we feel unsuccessful and therefore, unhappy.

I knew a sales trainer and speaker named Clint
whose happiness depended upon getting a standing
ovation. He was still trying to answer the question "Am
I successful?" and the answer was "yes" when he got
the standing ovation. A standing ovation made him
feel successful momentarily, until the next speech
where his very success was at stake once again. Clint
mistakenly believed that when he was good enough, he
would get more business. "Good enough" to him meant
more standing ovations. Because of his preoccupation

with "being good enough", he didn't get enough repeat business.

Clint was still trying to answer the question of whether or not he was successful. Had he already felt successful, he would have not had to spend energy trying to get approval via the standing ovation. Instead he would have spent his time and energy developing systems to market his services instead of trying to work on inserting one more joke, or one better pause between sentences.

Happiness Beyond the What Ifs

Clint has an erroneous belief that more work will equal success and that success will equal happiness. The danger in this philosophy is that we leave our success at the mercy of the "what ifs" in life. "What if" you never get the standing ovation, don't get the promotion, never lose the weight, ever have any free time, get sued by

> No matter what your current situation, you are successful in many ways, and the power you have for future successes rests in your choices.

the problem employee, your kid lives at home until he's 30, and you never figure out what you want out of life? Is there happiness beyond the "What ifs?"

Yes, if you are willing to take the success question off the table once and for all. It is at this moment that you have made a new commitment, the commitment to take full responsibility for your happiness. When you no longer question your level of success, you can then let go of all the "what ifs" that only serve to threaten your self-esteem.

This is when you will realize that you are already successful, all you have to do is choose to be happy and allow more success to show up.

Choose Happiness First

I'll be happy, and then because of my alignment, the right promotion will show up. I'll get happy then my weight will stabilize because I will no longer need to use food as a crutch or as a way to hide my feelings. I will be so happy living life that food will not be the highlight of my day.

I'll get happy and I'll spend my time the way that benefits me the most, and that happiness will lead me to the right job. As a business owner, my happiness will attract the right employees to my business, and together we will have fun and find purpose in the work we do.

I'll go ahead and be happy even if my kid doesn't graduate, because my kid has a right to experience life on his terms, and at some point, his decisions will reap consequences that will put in him the desire to graduate. Then if my kid does graduate, that will be icing on the cake. I'll be happy, and when I figure out what I want in life, that will be another happy day with a more focused direction.

I'll be happy when I present information and that happiness will more often than not be received with a standing ovation. But if it is not, the absence of a standing ovation still will not make a dent in my happiness because a standing ovation does not equal happiness. Only I am responsible for my happiness and it is my happiness that I experience every single day that confirms my success.

Because I am happy, I do things that happy people do. I smile, I laugh, I get together with friends and I strive for excellence in my work. I take time out for myself, and I eat healthy and exercise regularly. I'm interested in life and I find other people interesting. I ask for what I want and I let others decide what is best for them. I trust myself and I'm open toward others. When I make mistakes, I apologize and learn life's lessons. I am aware of my emotions and I feel what I need to feel to move forward in life.

It is great being happy, and because I am happy, I enjoy and attract new experiences and heightened levels of success.

Success is a Given

Your choices reveal your commitments. I challenge you to choose never again to question your success. Consider this notion: There is no competition and everyone is already successful. Can you prove this to be true? Absolutely.

If all you do is watch TV every single day without any goals, then that is what you have been successful at, watching TV with no goals. You have accomplished watching TV. There is no judgment and there is no problem unless you desire "success" on a different level and you are unhappy with your current situation of watching TV with no goals. If so, then all you have to do is make different choices and those choices will give you another kind of success. If you are stuck in a relationship that is unsatisfying, then you have

> Your choices reveal your commitments.

been successful sticking it out. You have accomplished "sticking it out." Celebrate that success.

If you want a different kind of success and want to experience love in your relationship, then you must choose different things to get that kind of success.

Do you want to reach a higher level of success? Success is a given if you know what you want, if you continue to put one foot in front of the other, if you know what it takes to meet your goals and if you are willing to do the work that is required. You eventually get to your destination, unless you have changed your path.

Success cannot be found by struggling on the journey. Real success is the result of being happy while on the journey.

I hope this book has provided insights on your success journey. I ask that you take the success question off the table once and for all. Own all of the success that you currently have and accept it without question. Instead of looking at any sense of discomfort as a lack of success, see these lessons as signs that you are on the right track.

Discomfort will come if you are not willing to take the responsibility, and I am assuming that if you are reading this book, you are indeed the type of person willing to take responsibility for your success. However, we have to make sure that we don't get confused by the illusion of what success is and what success is not. Success is not your background, your job, your income, or your beauty. Success is as much the joy you feel on the journey as it is arriving at your destination.

Realize once and for all that it is only the judgment of yourself that blocks your satisfaction. No matter what your current situation, you are successful in many ways, and the power you have for future successes rests in your choices. If you can look at your life as a way to learn the lessons of happiness, then it is true that your success is a given. Now that you have taken the suc-cess question off of the table, commit to your happiness and see if you make dif-ferent choices. Those new choices will lead to successes you never imagined. Your success

> Success is as much the joy you feel on the journey as it is arriving at your destination.

is a given, but your happiness is where it has been all along, it is now.

"The achievement of anything that you desire must be considered success, whether it is a trophy or money or relationships, or things. But if you will let your standard of success be your achievement of joy—everything else will fall easily into place. For in the finding of joy, you are finding vibrational alignment with the resources of the Universe."

Mark Victor Hanson

About the Author

Marlene Chism. MA is a communication and relationship expert who works with companies that want to stop the drama so that teamwork and productivity can thrive. Marlene also works with people who want to reach the next level personally and professionally. Marlene develops and delivers training for corporations around the United States. In addition, Marlene is the host of the web based, "Stop Your Drama" radio show where she interviews experts, authors and coaches dedicated to helping people create and live the life they want. The show is hosted at Women's Radio at www.womensradio.com.

*"Self-worth comes from one thing–
thinking that you are worthy."*
~Wayne Dyer

Additional Resources

ICARE Products

www.icareproducts.com

ICARE Products, the product division was born in 2003 when Marlene introduced the Builder's Series booklets, which have many uses for both training and marketing, and have been purchased by companies like NASA, McDonalds and Detroit Free Press.

Stop Your Drama

www.stopyourdrama.com

The Stop Your Drama programs evolved as a training program for managers who needed to learn how to manage themselves and others in the midst of rapid change. The program is based on William Penn's principle: No man is fit to master another who cannot master himself. Marlene's extensive research revealed what she experienced from over 20 years on the factory: Workplace drama hampers productivity and negatively effects the bottom line.

Character Builders

www.characterbooklets.com

Character Builders evolved in 2005 when Marlene Chism developed a booklet to compliment the Chamber of Commerce initiative to build a community of character. As a result of this product Marlene joined a collaborative effort with Character First! an international organization dedicated to providing resources to communities interested in promoting character. The Character Builder booklets are a vehicle to raise funds, promote character and provide character education for businesses. To see more about ordering, customizing or building a character campaign go to ICARE Products.

Attitude Builders

www.attitudebuilders.com

Attitude Builders Tool Box is a monthly subscription full of resources for those who lead others. Each month an electronic article is delivered complete with an employee version PDF to be distributed. Each motivational meeting in a box delivers bite-sized lesson that can be used immediately in any business, while giving the leader facilitation tips, quotes and tips that can be copied into e-mails, discussion tips and action items for upcoming meetings. The result is increased employee engagement, heightened problem-solving, better teamwork and open communication as well as intellectually stimulating meetings that employees look forward...meetings that create results! Click get your subscription or to learn more about the Attitude Builders Tool Box.

To inquire about a speaking engagement or corporate training for your company, call 1.888.434.9085 or e-mail marlene@stopyourdrama.com

What Others Are Saying About Marlene:

Marlene Chism should serve as an inspiration to anyone who would like to change their life. It takes a great deal of courage to leave a company that you have spent most of your adult life working for and start up your own. Marlene is a perfect example of 'where there's a will, there's a way. Her interactive, participatory style of speaking gets everyone involved and engaged. I would definitely recommend her to anyone who was interested in bringing a motivational speaker into their particular company."

Curt Lewis, Job Council of the Ozarks

"Your presentations were energetic, informative and helpful for all the attendees. We could have had you speak for a whole day and still wanted more!"

Dawn Uritescu,
Plastic Surgery Administrative Association Inc

"I have heard nothing but good comments. Your presentation was both educational and motivational. We will be able to make more conscious choices, communicate better, set boundaries and own our own stuff. You are an inspiration for all of us. "

Darlene Reed
Intercounty Electric Cooperative Association

"While we had a number of nationally known luminaries as general session speakers, numerous people told me that they thought you were the best speaker at the conference. Thank you for being part of AWC's success."

Pat Troy
Association for Women in Communication

Success is a Given
$14.95 US
$18.50 Canada

Shipping & Handling:
$4.00 per book)

To order additional copies of *Success is a Given,* please fill out the form below and return it via:

Postal orders: Mail to
ICARE Publishing,
1223 W. Linwood, Springfield MO 65807

Fax orders: Fax to 1.866.817.8217

Bulk Orders: Call 1. 888.434.9085 (Ask about special offers for quantity orders)

Website: www.successisagiven.com

Forms of Payment

Check: Make payable to ICARE Publishing

Credit Card   Visa___ Mastercard___

Name on card_____

Address_____

City, State, Zip_____

Phone_____   E-mail_____

Ship to:

Name_____

Address_____

City, State, Zip_____